I0711016

SUBJECT

" Through the Flames

We Survived Cancer"

You can overcome

1

By D.W. Jordan

July 22nd 2018

INTRODUCTION

If it be so, our God, who we serve, is able to deliver us from the burning fiery furnaces. And he will deliver us out of thine hand Oh king. (Daniel: 3:17).

Pretax:

Life is not as we think it should always be, and it does not offer us an easy route and clarity either. It has some surprises hidden in dark corners as we grow and learn from whatever it dishes out. Most times we learn life transitions in the future distant as we grow and go aside the changes.

Be that it may, we are forced to either face such changes, and challenges, while we wait and hope, what it may reveal in our favor. However; this does not alter what lurks in the darkness as we move fearfully toward some unknown end. Living long, has given most of us a new frontier with a glim of hope for some who maybe in wonder what lays ahead. Strangely as it may sound, one will be alarmed, and unarmed with such findings. These unexpected occurrence's steers right into our innermost being and leaves us shattered and bewildered of what is taking resident in our lives

FLAME #1

Frustration began to mount up increases while analyzing the meaning of the unexpected tidings. You now, are forced to acknowledge the critical options to attempt to mend these broken pieces. Hopeless we maybe, we must response quickly to take back what we had and forget this unexpected news. The slipping feeling began to move beneath our feet, foundations of our hope seem fast declining. You seem to be gliding in space as you are placed in the hands of someone or something new and unknown. Is this a curse, a lie, or a gift? The fear of the unknown has disrupted my daily routines I am amazed how quickly my body is null to response with the findings.

Our roadways we traveled were smooth and easy are no more and are interrupted by a "Not", has alter our plans as we search for resolve. We ask ourselves" Is this the doctor ordered? The prescription does not comply with what I considered for my life.

Being unaware, too much sun is harmful, and not enough rain causes droughts all these elements both serve as a positive and negative in nature. Too much of anything is not good for instance rainy days can destroy our crops, bridges, and roadways. Our homes once built in a secure place, we later on discovers cracking, in the walls well painted. Our roadways cave in, that leaving large sink holes, and pot holds, and we drive, and walk in our streets of life. We quickly discover things happen as our world turns and we are in search for tomorrow to be a brighter day.

We all love to consider the alternative, "the good, rather than disruption" That goes well with the "word "change? Pain does not register well with us, as we work very intensively to make sure we are safe and secure. Like most! We reach, for the summit peaks as we start our climb. Just ahead we see success, dreams, and hope in the future and within our reach. Then suddenly we find ourselves bewildered and caught in the snares that suddenly shift us to new levels or lows. Now we are in a tangled net of unraveling the entanglements of the threads which bind us together. We either works to comply with the basic rules for our achievements; or we broke all rules to get there without any disruptions or consequences for the place we called secure.

The question not often asked "what will happen if you fail or fall while in pursuit of all your heart desires and falls short making those accomplishment? All that you desired is interrupted by a Not? It is like being told over the hill is a large ocean and is not, a road, to cross to your beach and there is none. Out there! Somewhere, there is no ship, or boat, nor friends, or companion, no communication whatsoever. You are alone and void of any support in a deserted place where there is no help.

Through all your preparations, you'll done all you could do to prevent such outcome you are now experiencing. Yet; instead of getting what you expected, a negative result comes alone. You are forced to make due with what you have at your disposal and nothing else, but only hope. The call is echoed across our mental minds, be prepared" it says! The train is on the tracks and the time is nearing, make sure you have your ticket stamped "approved" when it comes to that junction. Life will present to all some crossroads or junctions, where we are forced to consider our options. Time has no limits; it is forever calling for change to some strange bidding to fill some empty void. "Too everything there is a season and a time. (Eccleastic: 3).

We have arrived at that time not by choice but, by living life and undergoing experiences that life brings to all the living. We now realizes, we are not the master of it." We must acknowledge a demand, a higher demands begging us to respond to a few questions. We are to reason with those demands, but never, think we have answered correctly. I must contend that He that asked the question has the answers. As a steward only, we work in the vineyard of life. It is wise to let Him answer his own questions for He is Sovereign. It is wise to say! Lord thy knoweth! Then sat, and watch, and learn, and discover the amazing things, He does in spite of our frailties. (Ezek.337:3).

Living is a serious matter, death concludes all matters! When you have nothing else left, God is enough. (Dr.D.W.Jordan).

A True Story

In the year of 1946; three year slater after I was born, I remember things that most folks would say, you were too young to remember! I dispute every word of that notion; Children minds can remember things they are not accredited for knowing. Like, the quite days playing in the yards with toy trucks, or tractors, while my sister making mud cakes with the red clay of Georgia can easily be recorded in memory.

Sometimes wild horses would come from some strange place unknown to me and my siblings! They just came rushing across the plain and through our play yard. You could hear from afar, the fast trotting, coming near, and nearer toward your direction.

Dad could be heard from the woods, or in the fields working would cry out! " horses are coming! Willie Mae, our mom, as he hollowed" "Get the children inside! Horses are loose coming in that direction. "Mom could hear what we could not, you know! She, would come running from the garden, or from inside the house" children! Come inside right now" she yelled".

We hurried and ran inside, and as soon as we got on the inside, the wild horses came right through the yard where we would be playing. That was exciting times yet! But dangerous, and yet it was a sight to see such large, and strong animals moving so swiftly crossing the plain.

We would look out of the windows, as they were speeding across the landscape, leaving dust behind moving so swiftly.

All I knew! It was a good thing to have listened to the voices or both our parents, they could see the danger, and save us from something worse. Those were times we would learn a lesson while playing in the yards or any where else, how soon our lives can be interrupted. We had to be on the alert always watching, for danger that would arise out of no where living on an open landscaped farm.

As I grew, and years passed, I recalled many situations that occur that brought some difficult moments into the framework unexpected. We had to manage, and deals withstand sudden changes even, though it was not ideal to me, but it was what it was.

My father, and mother decided had, parenthood planned long before I came in mind, and it was not my choice to have eleven children whom was destined to hard work. All I knew, it was a demanding challenge, every day for all the clans who was living at the Jordan's house.

I was born somewhere in the middle of that number the sixth child of the clan, mom, would all ways have mentioned that "I was gifted one" because I had a very vivid memory. I could remember the last argument they had, the last bone the dog had, and where he got it from.

I knew this! We all had to work hard to survive if we want to continue with our feet under the kitchen table. We all! Enjoyed the results from the labor we had contributed which produced our daily bread.

I remember the shacks we lived in on the farms, from one to other folks called them shotgun houses. We were to live there so long as we would share in harvesting the crops. We learned quickly, that the land was not free, there were things that had to be done if, you wanted to have a place, or roof over our heads.

I remember! Working and helping gather produce at the age of three or four, working alongside with the other siblings. We dug up the roots, of potatoes sprouts and vines; gather them for the long winter months ahead.

Mom and grand- mom! All worked in the fields when the crops were ready for harvesting. They worked intensely with whatever ailing, or heat from the sun, or rain from above, teaching us about what it's takes to survive.

The time came around in 1949, one of the luxury we enjoyed was, the radio. This is what our family did in those days. It was a wooden oval shaped radio which was designed with two connected battery like cable wires attached with a positive and a negative ground wire.

The wires extended out of the window onto a ledge

outside the house, with a large black ever ready battery logo. I remember this so well because, its icon had a symbol of a large black cat on the side with yellow eyes, and the label displayed power".

This was a good time to sit around with family and listen to the radio that revealed a grounding sound that sounded like it was the first invention of Thomas Jefferson himself, with very poor reception indeed!

The fight was with the famous Joe Louis, and Marciano, and it was being broadcast from the Madison square garden In New York City. The radio in those days was a big to do if you had one! You were considered well off. We could only listen to it when dad would say so," it was the masterpiece in the home, and no one touched it.

December 14th, 1946 has long gone, and I am now seventy years younger. You can now consider the years passed, and how old I really was then. We were what were considered 'field workers, and sharecroppers, sharing the crops made throughout the year with the land owner.

We had to work or, otherwise we would have all died from starvation. Work was mandatory for each family member on the farm work was year-round no part-time employment. Not all the time spent on the farm meant hard work, but what made it hard was it was constantly. There was something to do in summer, winter, spring and fall, all dad had to do was call.

Such a large family we shared some of the most rewarding moments being with each other. We had our own small town with family members' cousins, uncles and aunts. They were folks we could challenge to agree or disagree didn't make a different for everybody was wrong unless dad or mom said so.

We did not see many folks during the weeks because; we were too busy working on something from feeding the chickens, to slopping the pigs. The time came around when our cousins would come over and we shared together the usual things. Mainly we spent most of our time at church, and it was a special treat to go up town especially on week ends after a dusky long hard week.

Being good, awarded you the opportunity to go with dad, and mom when they went to sell produce from the

farm to the city folks. Items such as field crops, or other produce the town folks needed, this was the way our earned money to support the household.

Many times, I remembered when the weekends came around our parents would go up town as you say, and upon their return they would bring coke colas, and wieners, bread to make sandwiches, or hotdogs for us. This was a treat, we did not get many opportunities to visit stores every day of the week, as many do today, that was a luxury.

Those days were days, when we really got rewarded

for our hard work keeping things heads up on the farm. A nickel or two, awarded was Christmas all over again. We could purchase penny candy when the candy man came around selling gushing stuff.

Sometimes, we had punch board candy boards, whatever; punched on the board is what you would pay. Most candy bars didn't exceed five cents, this was great, our emotions were so high just of having, the candy man come to the house, was all fun.

It was a simple life where we lived with plenty of love, fresh air, and plenty of fresh produce, and cleaned environment. Our water supply was from a well dug by dad and neighbors, or we the family that could assist in the digging.

The love we learned was that of a law inaugurated from our parents, being enforced from the oldest, to the youngest member. Family love is a powerful thing in any family, it is that root, which holds and governs all families. From that nuclear we talk, and listen at each other issues, when the chips were down it meant all were down.

There was no next-door neighbor nearby like large communities and city life. Rural folks lived distance from each other, and yet, they were close enough to share in the common bonds of helping each other. Regardless whatever one was going through, we all felted it, and believed it our moral duty to share.

When sickness or illness came around, our grandmothers, or grandfathers, knew what to do with any problems that aroused among family members. Many of their arts were passed down to them. They, had all sorts of healing remedies, most was gathered from the forest. These were herbs, or plants, they knew worked from one generation to other.

One major formula they used was called Castro oil, which could solve any and every problem you thought you had. It was that kind of medicine that would make you vomit just from the smell of it. Sometimes if you had issues with sickness, you kept them to yourself for you knew what was coming. It was that white stuff in a white bottle that was thick it pours from the bottle like syrup thick and slowly pouring. Most time, they thought this was the cure for any sins, and illnesses, you had and committed. They would offer you coke cola, or something that would reduce that awesome taste in your mouth. It really was a cover-up, a well thought sour plan instead something better they could have given.

Moving from place to place the siblings began to grow, having other plans in mind, big ideas to venture away from homeland to escape such practices. I couldn't blame them either, things on the prairie was getting tight, and space was needed in a small shack.

The family began to get smaller, and time took its toil, with such a large family we, needed an overhaul to reduce the number. Mom did not want her children to work in such conditions, to seek better schools, not a one room school house with one teacher most attended. I agree! This was a good idea getting away from that hard work and a lifestyle not going very far. We had to double down to meet those requirements to advance ourselves for better schools, jobs pushing under difficulties seeking opportunities to advance our lives.

Many siblings left home and moved to larger urban cities for better opportunities where earnings were higher, however; leaving the nest was one thing, and leaving dad and mom was another, they relied upon each to contributed to keep the boat rolling.

Finally! most of us that managed to leave home, found our way through the world choosing careers, and new-found relationships, was a new world altogether.

Good for all that could leave because, that meant advancement growth, and stability. That however, could help those who were younger to meet their perspective goals they thought! A little there, and a little here, did not fill the gaps therefore it was a shortage. Yep! Things were a bit easier for dad and mom, after the house was emptying out.

Visiting home afterward, visiting mom sure made a great different when she complained about her pain. When monies were given her it seems all, her discomfort just vanished away, and it was a joy to see that big smile on her face.

Regardless! How many leaves the nest, parents still worries and is concern about their children. We salute our parents for the teaching and support they gave us, such a large family.

Both our parents were church goers and expressed great faith, a devoted loved for the Lord. Never! were they ashamed to let others know they knew Him. He (Jesus) was and has been their only hopes, and relied greatly upon Him through the thick, and the thin in difficult times.

It was their duty to live a testimony and not just talk about it. Their testimony was the life they lived as good Baptist folks did in those days. Over the fences or standing on the fences, they stood solid and had solidarity testifying to others from passed Sunday meetings.

My father was a good deacon, and a Masonic mason, and mom was eastern star sororities, and a member and deaconess, at church.

 These fraternities, and sororities, were considered renowned organizations for African American. To be a part-that of such fraternities, and sororities groups, was special. It was known then as it is still admired today to edify and lift minds to pride themselves of such a great history so often forgotten.

> Those times stood for something as many
> walked the walk and talked the talk as we say!
> "Neighbors helping neighbors" that they did
> in good times and not so good of times.

These and other organizations merged the black culture and communities tightly knitted families who thought of a better alternate than poverty.

These and others organization did instill in young men, and women to look forward to some higher standards.

But reading from the script, names such as teachers, and pastors, and church members was held high very learned folks you respected. These and other institutions gave structure to broken lives of both adults, and younger minds.

The moral standards were enforced by all small-town folks willing to do all that they could with little resources.

Time was of the essence, and things were taking its toil on our elderly brother which had big dreams, dreams of going to Hollywood and be a big star on the big screen. He thought he wasn't cut out for hard work, which was the job for someone else. Nothing was better than the dream of moving on from the farm and sail the blue skies to some land far away.

However, we all had that dream, but we knew all of us could not go, and by the way many of us were too young to venture away.

Personally! I thought he was a bit spoil jerk, and yes! He was an attracted young man you think? Mom also thought so it was so, after all he was her firstborn. Yes! She over protected him and encouraged him to go and give it a try somewhere, since he wasn't going to put in a full day work anyway.

Dad wanted things to go smooth, and thought he had the two elderlies four hands including his two to help out doing chores.

No! *To his surprise! One from the top two, were making plans to flee from the estate, searching for new horizons. Things were steering in his mind about leaving home without being caught. Yes, there was a stirring of opposition arising on the scene, and mom knew about it.*

Therefore, there was war talking from theater things were bending in favor for the elderly son escaping his prison.

It was her first born and she loved him and wanted him to be the man he wanted to be without consequences. What love moms have for their firstborn and spoil child? This he was as far as I was concern a brat at that.

Some relative was leaving going north, and that presented the opportunity for him to get aboard was on the planning board. This he did, he went to live in New York City for over fifth teen years, we never saw him again until he was thirty years of age.

Mom was happy, and dad was bent out of shape, he lost two hands that he could use are now gone far away,

◆ ◆ ◆

his was not good for the rest of us! There was however, another sibling two year younger whom dad sang his praises because; he would comply with the demands. He was not considered a handsome gay, but alright! I think he was the beloved of both my parents; he would work to satisfy them for he wasn't as charming as the older sibling whom we called Jr. He was named after my father, so it was proper to call him Jr.

From time to time would send a note from time to time, in the mail and mom would read, and share with us." he was doing okay! She would say! And we my get a chance to see him on the Ed. Sullivan show". A big dream of his becoming a movie star and be on the big blue screen. On one occasion I remember Mom, had all the neighbors to come over to watch TV to see her son on the big round television the night came, and Mr. Sullivan introduces his guest. If I am not mistaken in Georgia it was broadcast in the evening around eight pm, the neighbors gathered in one large room with us to watch the program. Everyone around the small town was summoned to watch mom's project assignment in force. Mr. Sullivan came and went and no! There was no Jr. to be seen on the show. We all dropped our heads with a smirked face in embarrassment, because Jr. did not appear and there was snuggles in the crown. We did not want mom to know what was on our minds, we all played it off, "Oh well that is it we swiped". Mom always had a response for most comments made regardless of whom made them. She burst out in the crowd and said, "He properly was on the show, but he was in the back mopping up the water that spilled." We all burst out with laughter". Finally, we got notice that Jr. was truly coming home for sure. A big dinner was planned and for sure he did arrive, and all was glad to see him, been away for such a long time. He needed work badly and dad was to encourage this-for he left with some unfinished business at age fifteen. Dad was working at a clay mine manufacture and thought he would like to work there for a while. He got hired, but the job did not fit his description, he still had soft hands, and still didn't have the skills to block from skinning his hands. The brother next to him had moved to St. Louis, and He offered to come and find a new career there. It was at a foundry company working with steal or making railroad cars. He worked there for a while even though he was in a mental opposition state of mind, while working there but, he did work.

Well! The time and day arrived, it was a certain day, and time, early in the evening unwelcome news came. In August 8th, 1974, I received a call from a family member stating that he was found dead in his automobile, not far from his place of work. I was summoned to come! to the city morgue to identify the remains.

What a chore? You do not ever want to be called to this kind of identification in your life to visit this kind of burning flame of disappointments ever. This was a flame unsuspected yes! All younger siblings cherish the oldest always, but never to be called on such occasions as this.

Entering The Morgue, And The Remains Being Unveiled My Heart Went To The Lowest Common Denomination To Have To Face Another Flame Of Disappointment. As It Goes! I Informed Mom, And The Rest Of The Siblings Of The Situation They Two, Could Not Believe The News. We Were Not Sure What The Cause Of His Death We Did Not Have An Autopsy Done On The Remains. This Was Very Difficult For Our Parents, And His Family, And All His Siblings And His Family. He Was Thirty-Seven Years Of Age So Young To Go, His Life Was Shortened. But! Thinking About It Later, We All Are Never To Young, Or Old To Have Life Events To Defame Our Good Moments, At The Dropping Of A Hat, Things Just Crumbles And Disrupts Our Plans.

Flame #2

Our, the elderly sister had moved from Georgia and found her resident St. Louis Missouri, her resident was with the second elderly brother, who also lived in the city. Therefore; he was willing to take both of us in for a while until we get our feet on the ground. I had come to St. Louis and lived with him for a while and had to move and find a new home for both of us for the burden with both of us was enough. That I did- found an apartment, purchased used furniture, and set up house for both of us. I was only seventeen years of age old when another fire was set off, and the smoke seem to have small bits of cambers being ignited. Things was changing in her personal life, things I knew very little of.

Little did I know what was taking place in her life, I had my own life struggles, while attending school and working a job at the same time? After getting home after work, my neighbors would inform me how the day had gone with her and her two small children. They would say! She has had some difficulties during the day however they were good people but nosy as well. She had two small children which needed her attention which she was not able to give for some reason it was unknown to me.' I started taking notice of her demeanor, and asking questions what she was feeling? She would say, oh nothing! I'll get over it" "you are trying to get over what? I asked! She says oh "nothing".

Being unaware of the word cancer given all due respect for those who did, things were whispered about it, but not often spoken is public square like it is today. However, the word had spread with the girls whom were a bit more informed than the boys. Not many people spoke about that subject especially free as it is spoken today on the news and each day. Obviously! Moms knew more about that than I did, and I did not know what to do to get her to band her self-inflicted lifestyle, dealing with her emotions and other failures. There were things changing back home and mom needed our attention more than ever with matters in the family. Being young and living in the big city working and going to school I really did not know what to do to fulfill mom's request to get her back home was the best idea.

Come back home? I said mom! What I am to tell her the reason we are coming home? Mom knew she loved her father and said "tell her daddy is ill! That I did, and that seems to have triggered some movement toward the idea it made things a bit interesting, toward leaving and making the move.

I discussed with mom and told her, I did not know what else I could do. She suggested for me to bring her home, so she would assist her through the ordeal.

That I did in 1966, I loaded my car along with her two children and headed home, and still she had her reservations to me was unknown. I knew she loved daddy and told her that daddy was very ill, and we needed to go at least see about him. That was the energy that motivated her and broke the camel's back now we could be on our way. We started out going down route three in those days; we had to go through the Tennessee Mountains with a broke down used car. It was a total broken piece of junk smoking like a freight train that burned, a lot of SPT oil treatment as a freight train going down the tracks. I was young and had been on that trip many times with my older brother, but this one was alone just the two children and the two of us. I knew ahead of us was a long lonely journey plus driving in a misfit junked automobile that could blow out any moment. I knew this was the only option I had, and I had to have faith and trust in a higher power with little money, and a little sense. I could take the challenge and complete the journey home from St. Louis to Sandersville Ga. was about twelve and a half hours straight through none stop.

We arrived at home in the evening around six am the following day, arriving in one piece. Mom came running out the house so glad to greet us and so was dad. Realizing the limited, and time was of the essence I knew it was going to be a swift transition and it had to be to return Saint Louis. I needed to give as much information about her I could we had to convey privately and personal that things would go as we had planned. Tired, from the trip I was falling asleep as the conversation continued listening and falling asleep as the conversation goes. I would attempt to keep my eyes open to justify why I brought her home and the children so, I wouldn't feel so guilty. We all knew, I would be leaving early the next morning early. I had to return for work in two days, and knew before hand, I needed to reassure her that all will be well, and I'll keep in tough.

This we did! From time to time inquiring about her conditions! Mom would say! She is doing fine and the next day or so, she would say...Oh! She's not doing so well! I would call her when time permits and talk with her about things back in St. Louis. I knew this was a place she loved and knew, and she knew I was a young minister of faith she, would say to me, brother! Keep praying for me! I would say" Yes! God is on our side.

She would ask me why I left her and did not tell her I was returning? I knew she would not want to go home but she needed too for her failing health.

 So, as time went on I realized I had done the right things and knew, it would convict me when I heard those words out of her mouth why?" I explained to her It was something I did not want to do, but it was for the best and little did I know, how right! I was after, it was all over.

I did not have the proper insurance and did not know where we could get it for her and there was not Medicaid or Medicare for most in those days.

Not many large black families had medical insurance anyway; insurance for catastrophe conditions and cancer just was not in question. Most had those scam policies for burial expenses but nothing for long term care.

She knew I was in the ministry at such a young age and she relied upon my faith to intercede for her and that I did the best way I knew how I wanted to see a miracle also.

She would ask me about different herbal ingredients she was taking that would help her withstand the pain and assist in curing the disease. I really didn't know anything about any herbal medication, I had heard about it through my grand-mother, and father, how at one time or another such herbs did react to certain disease.

This was as if ten thousand tons was placed on your shoulders, and the weight was so heavy we knew no where to go and how to get the help so needed. The only force we had was prayer, and faith that would comfort us in such times as those. After a long period of watching, and waiting she concluded in a quiet moment at home with mom whom had been through another storm. This was the beginning of a flame that ignited the family flames in April 1977. Cancer had struck and taken a life and we did not know how to deal with anything anymore it seemed

FLAMES #3.

All things considered and done the next two weeks, I received a call from mom saying; "Son! Your father was killed in a car accident today." my spirit went to its lowest point stricken with grief; it took toil on both of us, with such reoccurring tragedy. I did not know how we could do this again in such a short time our financial affordability was depleted, and we saw no way. Mom tried all she could to brake the news softly, but it came out with a voice of pain, and sadness. That really hunted me more and my family whom had just experienced a deep moment of grief, a flame that hasn't fully dissipated and, the emblems was still full of fiery.

I was pasturing a small congregation at the time they were concern about our state. The death angle was riding swiftly, and we are summoned to return to another fiery storm. It took all the strength I could mussel up to return and give support since I was the oldest son available to be there. I recalled my wife, and I, with three small children we could not leave them behind we had to go on regardless. A member of the congregation came to us and offered help for us. They said! Instead of driving, "We will give you and the family tickets. It was the first time we as a family were blessed to commute within an hour and a half to Georgia. We arrived into Atlanta airport rented a car and drove the rest of the way home the second time.

There we meet again on another unwanted occasion,

none of us had time for healing, it was a must do situation or just do the anyhow, that could bring a sense of ease to all at such an emotional moment.

The pain was so horrifying it seems our world was tarring apart, it was all messed up! "Where was God? Silently seeking answers from within, "It is more than we can bear". Yes! We do ask many questions whenever things are not in ourselves control. Was He angry with us? What is the message he is trying to convey? What are we missing?

On the faces of the children who wanted to understand seems terrified "what do you say, and what do you do? My answer speaking out loudly "God has a plan," we just do not know what it is He's up too something"!

I knew deep down within I could not turn from Him amid all that was happening, "When I thought good, evil also was present" (Roman: 7:7). I just knew we were experiencing fiery furnace moments as it seems to never burn go out.

 I remembered my mother already filled with grief cried out during the service" You! Went off and left me! Saying to my deceased father! But! I'll see you soon. Do you know what that is like? Hearing such defiant cry? Can you imagine what it was like putting away a son, a daughter, and a husband, all within a year and a half? Children are not to go before parents" they are to live to take care of their parents in a rightful old age.

Flame # 4.

Twelve years later! In 1992 May 3rd yes! It was Mother's Day, my youngest sibling was with mom who called me on Mother's Day around eight-thirty in the morning saying to me" Mom" has passed away, I said! You'll kidding? Aren't You! No, it's true she passed after getting up from bed and got strangled, and the conversation continued.

Mother's Day! I thought to myself...not true! I turned to my wife and told her the news you could see the hurt from her eyes she did not know what to say or think, I was speechless! Prior to preparing, to deliver my Sunday morning message to small group of hurting people dealing with their flames of their own.

I continue to prepare for worship service realizing the pending problems our church was facing financially they, I had needed me that Sunday. I had no substitute minister form moments like these emergencies I had to do the job and go it alone, while paining myself to be strong for the members who did not know.

I am lost for words to say and prayer seems to have left my lips, while tears started flowing from my eyes, as God granted me strength to get through that flame that burned so painfully in my heart.

I searched deep down within my heart and considered how quickly life brings news that changes the way we feel and think so swiftly. I considered how vulnerable we human creatures really are but dust just waiting to vanish away, one inhale of breath lacking.

Life hits us with so much we can only plea for help as we find ourselves helpless, disassociated, lost for words beyond our imagination. While this is not a good moment, but it can be a learning experience, for we can only do, and response to what has been given, not our favored choices, but this is the orders pending.

I questioned many times who ordered this menu? This was not supposed to be this way; I understood that life was in my best interest, granting me health and prosperity, and long jeopardy all which I live, and long for. But, no! Here come the judge summoning me to answer the call" Who shall I send and who will go for me? I had to comply "Here am I send me I'll go even If I cannot see my way.[1]

We have done all things right by living a certain life style; we are pretty well adjusted knowing how to deal with others, treating our neighbors respectfully. Doing our good daily tasks our desire to be subjective and be judged fairly and life should reward you fairly for your works.

Little did I know about life and how ugly it shows

its ugly face when we are at our worst moment. Even one of His noble sons wrote" It is good for me that I have been afflicted, that I might learn thy statutes. (Psalms 117:71). Is here I asked myself like Job! "Oh, that I knew where I might find him" (God). I wanted answers to these flames of fire that keep burning and no one knew where they start and who set them afire.

I cried out! "Life you are not fair!! When I desire sunshine you send rain, when I desire peace disaster come alone.

"For it is a fire that, consumes to destruction, and would root out all mine increase". (Job: 31:12). There is a fire that comes to all our lives that consume us and we cannot put it out and cancer seems to one of those fires.

Why don't you lighten up a bit? This is too much for me to handle come back later, after I have gotten some rest from all your undesirable injustice, and pain, and suffering.

For some reason life respond to me in the quietest moment saying, If I give you justice you will be dead already I don't go around handling out justice postal cards. My job is to give you mercy. Mercy! I responded! Who wants mercy its takes to long for it to response to my situation healing is what I want now, and not later.

I wanted to get back at life what it has done I was okay, without dishing out to me things I have no control of. I am working hard to comply with what I feel, and I do not feel able to handle this sudden change.

Others seem to get a past, and here I am dealing with quilt, suffering, pain, rejection, brokenness' it is not fair.

Why am I always getting the ruff end of the stick? And nothing good for me all is useless and going out of control? As if I was born at the wrong time in the wrong place.

For some reason life did not respond to me as I wished it should have? It was as if I said the wrong thing as it hurled another flame as if I was in some contest to earn a prize unworthy. I am innocent I know nothing about cancer and that I do know, is very little. Can't you see I am lost for resolution? No, no, you just want to give up, you keep Wheeling your fiery darts my way.

You just want stop, will you? I am constantly reminded of what you have done. My elderly sister was taken my father, mother; we lost our elderly brother what's next?

Flame #4,

The brother whom stayed on the farm worked to comply with all the rules until leaving home had moved to the big city of Miami Florida. He is the one whom had sent a ticket for me to come and visit him when he moved to St. Louis.

This was my way out and happy to be out to further my life and do something for the family. I really wasn't the one to take the trip, by brother a year younger than I were to make the trip. He just could not do that he went fishing without a permit and had to pay that fine fishing without a permit, and the lucky ticket felled to me. I was the lottery winner mom said. I was given the opportunity to come to St. Louis during the summer months at least.

I believe mom knew that I was not going to return, and she was blessing me on my way for she knew we needed the funds to help. When I arrived, it was such a smoky city large and amazing especially downtown I had never seen such large skyscrapers and cars, and businesses before. This was great it appeared I could make it here. People was working and going and doing things the streets was busy. All I needed was a job and that I was given after arriving in St. Louis, on a Saturday.

 I had a job waiting for me at a wholesale grocery company. Yep! my brother had gotten me to work with him he needed the help with five children anyway, and I needed a place to stay for a few months. I lived with him for a while until I got on my feet and that I did within three months. Out! On my own was a bit scary, but I geared up and faced the challenge. Yep,' I went around town searching for used furniture stores looking for the things I thought, I would need to set up my new apartment.

All this came to pass I completed my apartment and how proud I was. I also found a used car, so I could commute back and forth to work daily. I considered myself sharp and knew how to put together a few cents away, but little in brain power. Realizing, the cost of eminence of ownership of a new automobile, even though it was used, but met my needs. This is what happened when I purchased that little car I found in reading the news paper. It was a German car, "a Renault for sale for one hundred dollars" the article said, and that was just my speed.

I rushed out to purchase it had rusty spots that that matter it had a good running engine that mattered. That was enough! It was for me and my special friend anyway, a miracle happened for me. Gas was only about twenty cents per gallon and the care only held about ten gallons that would carry me all the week long. It was a small four seated that was perfect for me. There were three other guys working at the company who did not have transportation and need to get to work. I made a deal with them to contribute at least five dollars per week- person_ person, was cash in my pocket.

Would you not call this a business plan? a savage business plan. I had money left over for the week left to carry me over to the next week. It only cost me five dollars per-week to fill the car. This was a big transformation for me things was needed back home, and I took some of those funds and sent them to mom to help out with things.

She was proud of me and I was happy to contribute for Dad was doing all that he could and yet! there was more needed. I was on track again. Later years my brother becomes ill from time to time. He had not insurance from the company because the company did not offer that" but pains were throbbing in his head. I never knew of him being ill any time in my life, his health seemed to be quite well. One day his daughter told me, uncle! Dad has been taken to the hospital with problems in his head. I told her I will be at the hospital to visit him, and upon the next day I did.

I entered the room where he was taken I said to him, what are you doing here? He replied just some pain in my head bothered me. Teasing him I said "throw that pain away get up! And let's go. I was trying to make myself feel better, but I knew it had to be a major problem for him to be in the hospital with just a headache. Later my brother a year younger than I showed up.

I knew than it was something seriously was taking place. I had forgotten I was the one to inform him about the brother in the hospital. We discussed the situation over, and over again of what the doctors were saying about his condition. Time passed they released him from the hospital he resumes work but only for a short time. I received another call that he had reentered the hospital for pain throbbing in his head. He was diagnosed of having cancer in the brain this was not good.

Another shocking experience a large tumor was found in his upper cranium he needed emergency attention right away. The doctors came and informed the family of the saturation and what could be the final results but, nothing speaking of death. They had done this before and others has made well of the operation.
Therefore, they admitted him to operation and after the operation things seemed to have been going Okay. I was especially thankful and feeling good about things until the day came when his daughter called to tell me "dad is having pains in his head and he needed to go to the emergency room right away for observation. That

they did take him to the hospital and I went to visit him there.

 To my surprise he was being treated on and with tubs everywhere connected on to him. There is nothing anyone could have done but pray and trust God, which was my only reply to anyone who asked and were concern.
We as humans do what little we can do when visiting our love ones. We try to ask all the right questions not realizing how important it is to those who are facing certain illnesses. It is our only strength just to understand what cause and effects taking place with those whom we care do much about. In a true sense we are asking someone to fix the problem and that would give us some assurance all is going to be well and good. This is what we all want to hear when we love someone.

Boy! Nothing was better for me than, to hear those precious words "All is well" wonderful words and words of consolation and resolve. Not all the times these words substantiate what we desire, there are other words that takes their place in our lives. And that what happen "We have done all that we can do, and the rest is up to God and your faith. What a moment and what

a lost as of January 28th, 1998 He departed this life to another.

 As I mentioned before, "like just do not give us what we want. I not sure it gives us what we need either. This I do understand there is a learning experience that comes alone side of problems.
We must believe that life has a good ending otherwise we are lost in our efforts to continue to help build other lives and be clear about our mission on this earth if losing this hope, we are not humans and void of all

that is good.

Flame# 5.

Flame! After flame, just kept coming one after another, my beloved sister three years younger than I, I gave her a call just to say hi! She lived in Albuquerque New Mexico. Both she and I were very close, we shared some of the same gift of speaking, and music. She loved to laugh, and have fun, we would teas each other inviting a good old time going down memory lane or course, our Lord always come in the conversations.

She had come to visit me several times as I ministered the church in St. Louis, Missouri. She and her husband would drop in and share in the services. We all shared things about the good old days, like siblings do speaking about our bad times, and good. She loved St. Louis and was visiting us around the 4th of July celebration.

After leaving, they flew back to Albuquerque New Mexico. She had mentioned her condition to my wife doing her visit with us. Later news broke that she was ill, and that news was not good, we both discussed the matter and prayed asking God, for divine help and strength to intercede for us on her behalf.

In our conversations time after times she would speak of going back east which means! Moving back to Georgia, or South Caroline to live there, and that she could continue her ministry there.

As the conversation goes! I said to her, "you will go back east! From a dream I had had. Some day "you will go east' I said. From my dream, I've seen water flowing in that direction I said! I versioned water flowing in that direction speaking presumptive to her to calm and give some ease! I thought. We often spoke about prophesying in some of our conversations, just our conversation. It was just our talk, as we both understood where we thought that conversation was going neither she nor I knew the fulfillment of such notion.

Being not so clear of her situation, not much detail had been given about her illness. Soon, the phone ranged, my wife answered it. On the phone I could hear the emotional voice of my wife saying, O, no, oh, no! I knew then that the news was no good. My wife after leaving the phone said Liz is seriously ill and was being rushed to the hospital she was in a cardiac arrest going to the hospital.

I responded I will be getting a ticket and booking a flight out there to be with her! I said to her husband. A day later, I rushed to the airport and purchased ticket. After leaving the airport some way, and some how the rickets was miss-placed or lost. I rushed back into to the counter personnel could they replace the lost tickets? They replied No! Sorry! We cannot replace lost items.

I had to purchase another ticket to take the flight it was right after 911attack in New York City. I admit I was rushing and trying, to get there as fast and I could. After landing in Mexico, her daughter met me at the airport and took me straight to the hospital where she was.

Rushing to her room, she was lying in her hospital bed with all sorts of tubing and attachments, not realizing she, had had slipped into a coma prior of my arrival, she couldn't response to anyone.

Not good new! I was not able to communicate with her as her husband, and daughter, was in the room praying. I joined in the prayer meeting for a period as the doctors, and nurses, kept coming in and out making their rounds.

Another sister flight arrived, afterward her arrival we all joined together in conversations trying to encourage each other to stay strong, and to be loyal, and do all we can to calm ourselves, and others who depended on us, for information.

We would paste back, and forth on the floor, It was limited for us to do anything. She mentioned to me that she would stay a while with her and I could get back to St. Louis, with my family, since I had a business that needed my guidance.

I accepted the idea, and started toward the airport to aboard the plane, as soon as I went through the airport checking point; I received a call from my sister stating to me that "she has passed".

Later, I discovered that she also passed with breast cancer, the flames were getting higher, and higher, did it burn in my heart? Yes! Another sibling has gone on. a sense of helplessness, and hopelessness, gripped your hearts. In these moments one must take care not to judge anything but be quite and listen to what is being said from a higher power other than yours. If you know anything about suffering, and broken-ness, and divisions that happen in life, then you will understand what you need to do in times like these.

Her remains were flown back east as predicted back to be with the other siblings whom had gone on. We all were lost for words to call for the firemen to come and diminish these uncontrolled flames; we do not have enough water from our eyes to quench the fires.

Time went by so fast, the children has grown, and are able to carry on as it seems. Their faces seem to be asking questions! I myself could not explain deal-ing with the fear, and emotional brake-downs, were a bit much for family members grieving. I had little to offer in way of conversation on our drive back home after the service. At this point you do not have words to express anymore, I had to listen to whatever God was doing and saying.

Flame #6.

In the summer of 2004, addressing myself as a business man, a family man, and a father, and husband lightening strikes again! No! Not the man whom always giving out answers and consoling other? Yes! It is I, the lion among the whips. Turn away go from me! Am speaking to myself. No, no, not the one who does the God's talk? How this could happen to me and why? I have to say, I am married to an angle who keeps her eyes on me at my every move, and action. We have four children; three are married and one young son, on his way of seeking a spouse. My wife, noticed after using the bathroom I had reddish blood color after using the bathroom from my urination. She said to me "did you know your urine has a red tent about it? I had hoped to have flushed the toilet before she made her arrival but wasn't fast enough. I was command to call my doctor the following day to set an appointment and that I did. I go in for another checkup hoping all is well, as it usually has been after taking a yearly examination. To my surprise, the doctor came out and said! I need to draw blood for further testing. His assistance came out and drew blood, and goes back in the office, obviously they had the screening in house.

It took about half an hour to an hour, for the results came back with concerns. We sat in the office hoping that all is well, and we could go our way as usual. The doctor came out and said to me! you have a high PAS I want you to go see another doctor at St. John hospital, for an apostasy to be taken that we can be sure of our findings. Within a week or so, and after the initial appointment, the result returned from the doctor's office stating, "you have prostate cancer".

Now reality is setting in and I just said within myself, "Well it my time I can only deal with my faith and God to decide what is best for my life. We left the hospital in somewhat amazement. I could see on my wife face the concerns she was struggling with, I said to her "everything is going to be okay. I was thinking about her and my youngest son, and about leaving them behind and lot of crazy things began to set in. I knew my son was concern about his dad he was just fifteen years of age but, he really didn't understand.

My daughter who was older understood somewhat, and one of my older son was told whom what most elderly children does, say a little, or look amazed at you". I had to make some quick decisions, and want to get it done as soon as possible so, the flame of fear, and frustration, will not set in my thoughts.

I focus on things continuing as usually, and I will notify my church family asking for prayers to be offered up, for me and the family. I will never forget sitting down at the computer writing to my family things, I would like for them to continue doing if I must depart. It was at the right time and night time, when I could concentrate on what I want them to know. Mainly I want to secure my wife emotions as I knew; she was hurting and wanted to know more about this disease. I want them not to worry so! I started making fun of myself in the letter I was writing.

The day to have surgery the pastor came to have prayer with me prior of going to the operation room.
God would take care of my family if I do not come out okay. I spoke these words to them as they came to take me into surgery. All the children who were present had to get back to their work and only left my youngest son and wife, to wait the four hours for the operation.

After I gave my information they questioned me, and some how, I remembered no more I, was taken under by the medication given me. I remember I was awakening by my wife, and youngest son, standing over my bedside after the surgery. They were smiling, and had concerns on their mind how I was feeling? Or course! I was paining, and the nurses came in with demands take this! Do that! Turn over! etc. I had no other choice, I was in their control and was very hungry, and I let that be known. One of my siblings has flown in from Atlanta this was also comforting that she came. I knew she was much support to my wife to have someone to share with and discuss my condition with she had been with me in Mexico. Well! I must say I had another brother next to me whom also visited Mexico made his present by way of telephoning.

I thought I was going to take a rest at least for a week, No! No! I was to get out of the bed the next day and do the drills, "Walk the hospital Isles" I had a stomach bubbling inside as if I was going to explode. Now! I know the purpose for that humiliation walking! The gas built up from the piecing of the body. The next morning my doctor came by to check up on me and does his usual bedside duties. He told me that had gotten all the cancer of the prostate and I could go home, "do no heavy lifting his orders". There were moments thoughts came to mind of what lies ahead. The feeling of not being strong again and how would my wife deal with my condition after the operation. Would I be normal again? Have the same functional and desires as I once had? Well! After it all was over and having an understand spouse things went quite well. I learn however: what is the most valuable thing in life, and that is the care of someone who cares for you, when all other things matter less. As men we fear a great deal of things when it comes to our sexuality. However! Important that it may be to some, it is not the last thing on earth that bring you comfort. You will never know unless you understand life, and when your life has beaten all odds against you and you cheated death. Many men I've met that had prostate cancer were reluctant to go and to get the proper check ups so badly needed. They often say, I'm going soon, or things are going to get better when they are not in most cases.

African Americans men must start doing some home work since the diseases are rapidly among this culture. Not that is not among Whites Americans it is there. Yes! I know what you are thinking concerning your manhood, and sexual matters. But! As I often say! What about death and what will you do if you wait to long? Many heroes passed trying to override the requirements of getting to see the doctor and wind up in the mortuary months later. It is a matter of fact that cancer carries no pain and sometimes it is difficult to detect it unless; you get to your Neurologist in time to advice you properly. I did not fear of loosing or becoming impotent. Being total empty of good, sound judgment, is deadly to you and others you love. Family can give tremendous support if they are concern about your well being. And if you have a family member or spouse, that cares about you then, listen and do the right thing. This is what I call being a real man who takes the moral responsibility, staying in control always with your physicians, and others who understand your fears, and rejections.

I chose to live, and sweat not the small things in life, to be alive, and live to see your grand children, and children is worth it all. Plus acknowledge the life, the miracles life God has given you, is to live again is reflect upon," How great thou art? Therefore! Some battles are not to be fought by you, they are given to learn from, and share with others.

This is a humbling experience when your life is threatening by cancer regardless what form it is, stay focus. You would not be so easily to judge others not knowing what they are experiencing daily as we go through life. You will be careful what you say, and do, once you have gone through such experiences as cancer.

On one occasions, our late president Abraham Lincoln once said" I feel sorry for the man who can't feel the stripes when they are placed on another man's back". knowing this as he goes his way to maturity and grows in grace. There is mountain never too large to be graded down" is my quote there are things in this life will challenge your faith. You will encounter the enemy attacks on all sides to bring you down, I had the catchier on my leg in which to release at night times.

 Conditions like this, one has no control of, my body fluids had to go somewhere after the fact where the device was the device was inserted from the bladder for that purpose.

We were in the process of moving out of state, and things were pressured after selling our home. I wanted to leave St. Louis just anywhere where I could feel the warm sun. I felt cold at times as if my body need heat, the city itself looked dark, and cloudy to me. I mentioned this to my wife I not sure she understood for she was actinically involved in many things closing school and making another change. Not often we appreciate our spouse like men should. The house needed packing for the moving, the usual things families does to meet that time cycle.

I made a few mistakes alone the way by lifting things, I should have not, and paid a price for that stupid error and was informed by my doctor. Just sometimes in our lives we as erotically egg heads, just spills our brains out of socket.

The doctor said, I could ride when we leave within a month after the operation, but not driving, and that I should stop everyone hundred miles to stretch. That commanding order came so, there wouldn't be a blood clot sitting in one place, for such long time. The day came when the moving vans arrived to make the move out of town. Our youngest son came to do the driving to help mom, and I which was a kind jester on his part. I realized though, it was hurting for him to see us leave but, happy also by this he would be free of both of us.

We stayed in Mississippi for three years until Katrina came along and blew us back toward St. Louis. The place was very too hot anyway; to much heat I thought I needed. I must admit, I was following into liking the place away from it all recovering. I knew for sure my body was being healed, as time moved forward or course, we needed a church home to attend.

As we visited a few, we came across The Ridge crest Baptist church in Madison MS and found it to be a wonderful growing family church.

Realizing he had been our refuge and strength in times of my troubles. We decided to make the move back to St. Louis, it was not all about St. Louis we missed, we had a daughter and a son with grandchildren was the major reason we wanted back in if they allowed us. I had to have medical follow ups often and my doctor seems to be the best one I needed that gave me the reassurance I needed.

After such operation within a year one must return to get his yearly checkup and be released from the doctor's care in a ten-year observation.

I was spared by God's grace to still have my life and in pretty good health. **I wrestle with silent pain, pain of the unknown. However; I concludes in my mind whatever flames may come my way, I rest my case that I survived with a new perspective.**

Flame #7.

While we were preparing to move back to St. Louis, from Mississippi we lived there for three years after what we called retirement not true! We both found ourselves back at work I was in retail with a large chain departmental store and so was she. In August 2007 while at work around lunch time, I received a call come in from the manager "you have a call" I did not think anything else sometimes it could be a customer but not usually.

My wife was on the phone saying, "I would meet with you for lunch, I will pick you up! Not as usual- I would drive my car and we would meet up at the place preferred. After which the store manager came to me and says, "Just take your time you don't have to rush for lunch".

That's strange I was thinking as I was leaving the store, this has never been said before, I thought I had won award for good service in attendance or something of the like. No, no, I went from the building my wife sitting and waiting in the car. I stepped in and sat down, she asked me how am I feeling? I replied I'm okay! Being married over some forty years- you know certain looks that says a lot about moves, and actions and reactions. I looked on her face there was a strange look- an amazement looks on her face.

I asked her what's up. She said your sister called and said-, your youngest brother was killed today" my heart dropped, I think I said-You'll kidding! Then I asked her "How"? I had just spoken to him two-week prior saying, "you take care of yourself meaning with his medication he suffered with diabetes and need insolence every day to eliminate dizziness, and other issues.

I immediately took my cell phone and called to Atlanta trying to reach my sister to get clarity of the situation. She answered the phone at the hospital where he was being treated. Then she said! He did not make it, he is gone. This was very painful and hurtful; no words could explain what the feeling. I took the day off from work trying to get all the details possible so at least I could get some thought as to how this could be! I had just spoken to him about some things with his best friend sister, how they should work together on things since they were close neighbors and rented together.

On the road again headed to Georgia and meeting up with my next younger brother traveling from New Jersey we met up in Atlanta to trail each other home. As we were going toward home, the news reporter came on from within Atlanta saying "A few days ago some gentlemen were on a certain highway and was struck by an oncoming vehicle and was killed- I was hurting and that made it a little worse headed on route 17 toward Tennille, Georgia his birth place and where the funeral was to take place.

I understood he had gotten on the interstate 75 in Atlanta on his way driving, and for some strange reason he was driving in the wrong lane facing coming on traffic. An eighteen trucker ran into him head on accordingly to the police records. The flames just kept burning over, and over. As usual we made preparation for his remains to taken to the funeral home in Sandersville, Ga. There are now six siblings taken away for reason or another. His demeanor was good he loved to perform for children as a clown for many occasions he called him bobo the clown. However! Being the oldest and being far away most of the time we had little association as time went forward. We the family made the best of it that we could, and he was laid to rest.

Flame #8

The sister that I called to get information concerning our youngest brother incident is now in the hospital from the accident. The word was being shared by the oldest sister who remains today, that she had pancreatic cancer. I heard the both speaking about the illness, they as usually argue as sister does from time to time, about getting in each other business. I know this! For I had connected them on a three-way call saying" If I wanted anyone to know about my condition I will tell them myself!

She had a strong personality and as always, spoke her mind. She had visited me when I was in the hospital, as I was recovering from prostate cancer. After that discussion later I want to know more of that conversation because, we have a history, and I felt I needed to know if there was anything I was left out of? She would call from time to time we would talk about most things, I was yet curious however, about their last fussing agreement is what I really wanted to discuss.

She was the one that was very private for she had been a single parent for a long time. When in Atlanta we would attend church together and share in a big way like dad and mom once did. Hearing those good old hymnals, they sang, and the shouts that came alone with the African American spirits, just took me back home again. She had three children and we loved them and tried to glean information from them. There was not much we could get from them either and one of her children was a nurse.

As time went forward, more and more news began to circulate more and more came out about her condition. She would say to me! I am going to visit the doctor today, "say a prayer for me she said". I was honored that she asked me and in other words she was telling me something was going on in her life. She was making her rounds visiting all the siblings she could knowingly who were sick. I put that much together after rethinking over things.

Later her condition began to be worsened and being distances apart there was still little information being given out about her. I was so swiftly that the news came that she was placed in the hospital for a short period, and soon placed at home with a nurse making visiting every day it seems. Finally, we were told she is in

Placed into hospice care, Wow! Was the only thing could come out of my mouth meaning God what is you up too? "Are you there? Are you listening? Why? Why? Was the prayer I was asking? Speaking with her many time prior she would always say "all is well" I was encouraged she displayed a faith not crying or acting in some strange manner. She went through her life as if it was not in her hands, but in someone much larger.

She had spent much of her time caring for others whom was ill as she visited the hospitals, and homes, when she considered herself retired. Finally, the words came from my brother a year under me saying, "You know she's in hospice's care and not doing so good. I said to him I will get my ticket and go there to be with her while I can. That I did when I arrived in her home her children and realities was sitting around having conversations. I spoke and went straight to her bed calling her name and saying "I am here, how things are going with you.

In her condition she replied, "The best I can"! I am the medicine man. I believe in the book of James chapter 5' and verse 14") "anointing them with oil and the prayer of faith will save the sick, and the Lord will raise them up" that were enough for me. I put all who was in the room out, so we could have our space together.

They had been there all the time and I had not". She and I were in the choir at church at an early age and we would sing an old song, "Lord gives me two wings". I asked her will she help me sang that song? She replied yes! We did that, and it gave her so much courage. I asked her to allow me to anoint her with oil and she said okay! That I did. We continue our discussion after a while and she said I want to get up and go where the others are! When I arrived, she was in bed feeling down and out, now she is asking to get up, wow that's great! I am thinking to myself! Look what the Lord is doing, she is up and walking! Praise the Lord I said. All that was in the room seemed amaze she was up, I knew I did. It was getting over in the evening and I had to catch my flight back to St. Louis. As I was being taken to the airport I received a call that she had passed away. By now you know the drill; back to Sandersville to celebrate her home going at the Tennille, Grove M.B. Church a large flame of fire had followed prior to all these flames...

Flame #9

As I mentioned prior the flame continue blazing high and higher. I never thought of how rapid these flames blazed. My thoughts like any normal family may think. With all the devotion and love we share, we looked to grow old and enjoy each other for a long time seeing our grandchildren finish school, get married having a full life. You never know what a day will bring. For a long time, we had another younger sister whom also was a diabetic patient. When visiting her in Atlanta, we would converse from time to time about thing that was concerning her and family. I knew she was paining and had suffered much over time, and the passing of her brother had taken place that she loved very much. We decided to keep that information privately for we thought she had had enough pain and suffering, in her life being a diabetic patient.

 She had three children, three boys in fact who has grown up raising their families. I remembered them as young and very active full of life. When I saw them again, they were l grown up with families and moving on. Their mother has been through many life ups and downs, just keeping her head above the water. Some folks do not realize the suffering with that disease. Mom knew this prior to her death, and she would say when she was acting strange..." she! Has sugar! That was the old school many used describing diabetics. I would visit her in the hospital when in Atlanta, and she was not able to see her best friend, the younger brother called Bubo the clown" pasted and went home. We really didn't want her to know being in her condition.

It was after a while before she was told by the youngest brother, whom was closed to her. I don't think' the news influenced her when she was told later. Leaving her in the hospital on our way heading home to St. Louis, I was thinking of all the burns, and smoked imprinted, that was on our hearts, and minds, as we droved on our way. There was no way to clearly explain to anyone, other than family members, what we have encountered. Despite her condition in a declining state and could not remain much longer. The struggle was too difficult, and painful everyone seems numb, and acquainted with grief, and sorrow! Like our Lord. It seems nothing that could change the course, or quench the fiery flames, flames, after flames.

 For me! it was the Holy Spirit that kept my wife, and I, strong through it all, the children were wondering what's going on? We notice, they were lost for words, and wondering what is taking place. Despite it all, they remained supportive with what they had, to comfort mom, and I, through the ordeal.

That was rewarding to see! When the chips are down to see the resilience in their hearts and thoughts. All our tears seem to have empty themselves, and we needed a recharge from the flames physiologically. Time is of the essence to reflect and to contemplate, what, and when to address our emotions. This went on for some time, as we discussed issues how we may put the broken pieces together? We are now returned to Lake Saint Louis, from Mississippi. I had the opportunity to work again in retail upon my return, after being there a short while I, became top brass, to salesmanship. I become top sell person within the store which gave me some motivation, and a new purpose.

I had gotten my results of my cancer; the news was great and only required for me to return only once a year for future visits.

Flame: 9

Well! In January 2015 my wife and I, was taking a joy ride and she mentioned that she wasn't feeling so well. Let us go and speak to your doctor and see what she thinks, I said! That we did, upon the visit at he her oncologist who examined her, the conclusion was, we recall, "Nothing found to be concern about" she stated.

However! We decided to get a second opinion from her medical doctor whom, told her she would

Send her to another doctor for a second opinion.

Therefore, the result came back and was told she needed to see another doctor for more comprehensive analogical results.

I took her to take a breast exam from another physician which was credible in her research. After two or more visits and being released until farther notice to wait and see she, told her. About two weeks of waiting!

I was at work, the phone ringed she called crying- the only words she said to me, "come home! I have cancer". This was not good news I quickly stopped what I was doing and knobbed to my manager said, "I must go they found cancer" and she needs me". Getting home! She was there with her head on the kitchen table with a frighten look on her face. I said to her everything is going to be okay! The lord will have mercy don't worry everything will be okay. If I am not mistaken she had informed as many of the children, she could. After all, that she couldn't do my daughter who knew quite well how, to get the job done. I have gone through this process I, came through that flame of fire, I said.

Regardless! Whatever! You say to someone who has not gone through that, "cancer" you need to rethink it again. That word means to many and most of us" the end" of life as we know it. We think the end of help has ended there no other reasons move forward any longer. It's easy to sit and talk about someone else emotional issues not having it yourself. It's another thing, to have someone closed to you to be affected with that disease. At those moments, you do not know what to do and how to perform certain things.

You don't know whom to call and chat with as; you search for answers and results. This is not wonderland of joy, and happy hour, knowing there is something in your body that can destroy your life. Your world is turned upside down, and things are not going right within. a few seconds it seems your life have been stolen from you, a thief has broken in and took everything. For the most part it has been a death sentences for most of my siblings, and nothing you could do to calm the storms. But! Deep down within my heart I felt God was doing something amazing in her life. I will never forget I told her, "You are going to be okay; God will take care of you.

That was my hope, and belief in her faith as we join in prayer believing God has done for both of us something special. Still you are hoping against hope, in many instances where sometime the enemy wants to get in through the channels of your thoughts. His great desire is to kill, and to destroy and do not look for a miracle. I would wrestle with that thought over, and over, how deep the vein has traveled within the family? I would sometime say things I was not sure of. I said them anyway, I kept my faith in the eternal power, I knew she wanted me to be the rock amid the storm.

I had pastor many churches, and claimed healing for so many others, "Why can't it work for us? Finally, her visitations become more, and more, for different doctors for examination. We had to make back to back visitations in one day, from one place, to another. She was very emotional about each visit and, had a ton of questions every word meant everything when spoken. Simple things you had to explain, and sometime what the physicians says, does not register well you are rushing for a quick good report. I must say, she demonstrated a strong will, taking it all the way to the bedside at nights we prayed.

One thing led to another, after another, one doctor saying one thing, and another says another. We tried to understand the best we could and even then, we sometimes got it wrong. Sometime, nothing has clarity, nothing is understood, and everything seems to be going the wrong direction. I was getting on her nerves searching for answers how to fix it "what to do and how to make things better. We had a pet dog which needed much attention as a child. In process of time, we were told she needed to stay away from the pet during this time" the dog had to be removed from her presence.

There were certain conditions had to be met on all sides from the doctor's office. The children who lived nearby had their family responsibilities they are allowing whatever time possible to visit mom. I have a job to maintain at work, and the needs to be presence with her as much as possible. Things like this are important to the sick person, and sometime saturation works well with some and others not so well. I desired for my schedule at work to be change, this did not go over so well for, it was about the money for the company. The real insensitive issues began to surface I had some days that I could take, use and that I did to just be there.

Our world had stopped for a season; time is of the essence for us to discuss matters of keeping thing afloat on the home front. We had a wonderful church family from our Sunday school department that offered support. They made visits, prayed, prepared meals knowingly that I was alone which was a God sent by their support. We had built a strong relationship with them that she enjoyed and loved being a part of. They got the wind of her condition I must say, and they came to the rescue at the right time. When you are a senior, all kinds of illnesses from one thing to another began to occur.

Many that learned of my wife illnesses went out in full force to assist in ways beyond imagination. The Family at First Baptist Church O'Fallon Mo did a mission for us, that was God sent. I could cook somewhat, I learned it from being the middle child of eleven siblings. We all had to have some skills everyone had to pitch in to make it happen. It came handy to my family, and very important in a marriage.

There are so many things that arise that a man should learn what a wife; (woman) has to do that is taken for granted by husbands. I gave it my best, not a perfect housekeeper but mom's taught skills began to work. Sometime your best is not received from those who are suffering, the food taste horrible, and waxed because of medication. My wife has always been a carefully crafted and decorative person always in matters of the home. As a caretaker, there must be an armor equipped individual with thick skin to comply with the orders given. When we talk about putting on the whole armor of God, nothing is short of that statement. "Wherefore, take unto you the whole armor of God that ye may be able to withstand in the evil day, and having done all, to stand. Ephesians 6:13).

It really felt like our days were evil, and some strange things were happening that usually do not happen to people of faith. There are times your faith will truly be tested, if you really trust in your God, discouraging moments will arise. Cancer in my family really felt like evil had gotten the best, you will ask the question! God, where are you? Like the patriot Job when he lost all his family by the enemy that had taken away all his children, cattle, sheep, everything he own. "So, went Satan forth from the presence of the Lord, and smote Job with sore boils from the sole of his feet unto his crown. (Job 1:7).

Your mind is full of all sorts of thoughts. You consider how can you keep going? You don't have an answer why this is happening, especially to a spouse, or even a small child. What do you say, and do, when cancer strikes someone close to you?

Soon, the day came when she had to and get her operation on a Monday on 5/15/15. The appointment would early in the morning at St. Joseph hospital.

The pastor of our fellowship showed up and had prayer with us which brought much comforted us. She signed in, and we waited for her name to be call and that came quickly. She was taken to waiting room where nurses were making preparation for those who will be going to the operation down stairs.

I sat by the bedside praying as we were talking over things about the process, and treatment, knowing she was nervous, and so was I. That was like a lamb being taken against it will to be carried away without it's will to help itself. I recall the day when I was being taken on the flat bed being pushed toward the operation room with the antiseptic in your arms toward the operation room. However; she was polite and practical a professional making ready the anesthetic for the operation. There was a great deal of medication she had to be given, I kept telling her you are going to be alright! She would say! I know, she contented ask the nurse will all go well? The nurse says "very soon everything will be fine; the doctor will be arriving soon to administer your medication. Soon after that statement the doctor came and as usually asked her "how you're doing?

She said okay!

She began to become a little dizzy from the medication you know! What that does to most patients. She had many questions seeking reassurance I must admit; my heart was a bit racing as well. She has always had a fear of riding elevators and I was trying to tell her, it's a cake walk. Even the nurse says there's nothing to fear you are in God's hands. The nurse offered prayer for her and both of us as she was getting a bit sleeper from the medication. Just before she was taken down the elevator my daughter came in a minute or two, before she would be in the operation quarters. Hi mom! You okay? She said yes, I'm alright.

By the time we got to the elevator, her voice began to fade more and more being taken to the lower level for the operation. We were given direction where to stay, while she entered the operation room. When we got to the waiting areas, my daughter and I entered where many others waited. I noticed they had on the wall an electronic board that displayed different colors to let us know what is taking place in the operating room. There was refreshment down the hall; I kept going there for goodies that could calm me down a bit. I would get up and pace sometime watching the board changing. It was a small family meeting with my daughter, and another special friend whom my wife and she had had close ties as friends. She arrived with a goody bag of goodies even if I had much sugar already; she had more of chocolate cookies.

One thing for sure my daughter and I were having a sweet party overloading with sweets, eating our nerves out. The operation lasted about an hour and a half this was a short! I said to my daughter. Yes, it wasn't long, a few minutes later, it came over the public-address system she is now being taken to the recovery room. After the operation her doctor met us in the waiting area and assured us, "the operation went well" and she will be taken to the recovery. Right then, I name the doctor, Dr. Zorro, this wasn't her name, but she was very puncture and professional. She is noted to be, one of the best doctor at SSM facilities also pinned on her wall plate. I had prepared to stay the night with her over night because, I knew she did not want to be alone I knew this since we married.

Throughout the years, we have practice to be presence as much as possible with each other. We were called to visit her in the waiting room, as you know a person just coming out under sedation do not need to be disturb right away.

By the time she went to the recovery room, our youngest son had arrived, along with my next to the oldest had arrived from Texas. Our oldest son was in Atlanta which desired to come but was advised to stay for mom would be going home the next day. My oldest granddaughter said to me "When grad-mom gets out! Give her a big ice cream cone. It was early in the morning the next day she got her final offer to stay or leave, we chose to leave. When we left we went out to lunch and did eat ice cream how right our grand daughter was. It was like nothing has happened we laughed and had a wonderful lunch.

There were many other testing needed we start hearing the word like chemo, more blood work, we need more information. Prior to getting to that point she had to visit all kind of doctors for all kind testing. Date setting for visitation with another doctor is not easy to follow up. I admit I was not a good record keeper she would ask me to do I remember the date she was to be at certain places. I must admit my mind was cooked I could only think of getting her fixed and back running as usual big mistake I thought. That would be the norm for some other cases, but for something like it is a serious matter.

You have to think of the emotional factor what a woman may feel losing that part of her body. Questions would be asked by certain friends of hers "how D.W. feels about that? They did not understand it was not about me, but her health condition was most important. Sometime people can think of the simplest things which may matter to some however; with both of us it was about survival. What really mattered was, making sure we are track for a complete recovery. One may think that having any type of cancer is light on the mind. Take it from those of us whom has had the condition tell you. It is not a cake walk in the park; it's a journey to somewhere unknown. It's a path the only the individual can walk.

If those people do not have a leaning post to lean upon during this flame, it is a lonesome road to travel alone. Let no one tell you, you can do it alone, no! We need someone to be there for support even just to listen to your complaints. When I had gone through with my operation and thinking it would be easy sailing, it was not. But being who I am "a man" you know, and having the faith I do, I must say I think I held up well. My wife however, thinks I may have lost a few screws from the process. After looking back afterward I may consider she was right, after seeing her situation and the scares it left.

Both of us has used our knowledge and our pride over forty-six years of marriage, has displayed our man and woman abilities as a challenge toward each other. But, wait until you face the real challenge such as cancer, soon you will learn the art to drop your pride and go for the ride. Wherever, and whenever someone tells you and lead you, you will go and do. You do not know whose hands will be your miracle worker, your counsel, and your guardian angle. Both of us as believers at least, could sit back and look at what was taking place in our lives.

I truly must say of all the times I visited the hospital facilities, I saw profound support will all the staffers. It is just amazing how the nurses, doctors, and even the janitors and services people, all are jointed together working for the good of mankind's survival. If you do not get this message while in good health, you will get it when there is nothing else left all your strength is limited. Not all the times one will acknowledge humility, as they go through a deep concern as cancer, many are self sufficient they think! Others see it as an opportunity to recover.

One may or may not consider people as a tool of God's provision when they are ill. We knew who our refuge and strength in our troubled moments has been. Grant it as we may! Living and seeing the passing of my siblings and asking questions in my personal life about why! The answer does not come that simple. If you have never known the power of God and how sometimes he doesn't always respond to our requests the way, we want Him too. Obviously, he has a plan we just don't understand, or would not like to admit that we are creature destined to deterioration and become bankrupted.

We have that choice to choose whom and what is works in your life either faith, or fate. Any individual should not be forced to consider making a life decision without making a personal choice who should reign over their lives. Even God is not in the business of forcing his creatures to comply with the rules. There is a law that we all may consider It is not the babies who are crying, saying save me, it's those of us who are aware of our destiny. We are the ones fulfilling our dreams, and desires, to use up life as we choose concluding we have no consequences of our thoughts.

We have the power within to choose life or death, is in our realm and reach to act independently. the responsibility to admit we creatures are probed to limitations, and failures is a matter of fact, a part of our existing here on this earth. If we desire to travel back to million of years and talk about evolution and we evolved from some thing or whatever. This is so simple for me about,

things of life as the bible state in Genesis's 1ˢᵗ. chapter and verse 1. Says "In the beginning God" that is enough to say how one would like to deny or clarify the term "In the beginning". Except it or break it, if you can erase it from your mind if you can. Go back and take away your birthday the day your mother conceived you, and you have life as you wish. Take it all back, you don't deserve it, and you don't appreciate it either, and your mother has contributed to you your life. Either we had a father, and mother, or are we void of both parents and we evolved alone? We owe no respect, nor are we liable for any purpose or cause do you affirm. In this life we are summoned to make a "clear choice", to except a divine record of the creation are do we chooses not too. "One writer stated, "To be or Not too be". "Make me to understand the way of thy precepts; so, shall I talk of thy wondrous works. (Psalms119:27)

It is good for me that I have been afflicted, that I

might learn thy statutes. (Psalms: 119:71,).

My wife and I have experienced a personal relationship with our faith in a true God. It is not that we survived that matters so much. It is if we pass from this life as we know it, there is a better place awaits us. God has a plan for our lives all that trust Him will be confirmed. "Inasmuch, then, as Christ hath suffered for us in the flesh, arm yourselves likewise wit the same mind, for he that hath suffered in the flesh hath ceased from sin. That he no longer should live the rest of his time in the flesh to the lusts of men but to the will of God. (1Peter: 4: 1, 2,).

We therefore; are giving our testimony of what we are thankful for, to tell others of the goodness of God.

We are confirming too you who are going through cancer do not feel you are alone. There are folks who are willing and ready to help you in trouble times.

Finally! the day came, that the word "chemo" came alone. The word began to increase more and more in the conversation. Now that's a challenge I thought to myself. Later, she questioned it also in many sessions with the doctors.

They handled the case very sensitive and giving as much information they think a personal could grasp. There were a lot of whys to ask about! Why this? And why that? This is a task even for the nurses. and doctors on a daily task.

I suppose if you don't understand and why

should you? After all it is not your body that has to undergo the treatment, questions should arise.

Believe me! There were many things no so simple and chemo is one of those things you should be concern about Yes, your life is at stake. The day finally came as we went to the medical center, where there was a host of people sitting in a room with tubes attached to their bodies.

You are introduced to Scott, Bob, Mary, and Sally, all different circumstances and conditions. There are those sitting enjoying the moments, and those eating, and those who are sleeping, and those who does a lot of things.

It took a while to get to know your neighbors within the facility and to ask the question about, what that red stuff you are be administered? The nurses would come alone dressed in their heavenly attire with long needles, and big smiles on their faces saying! "How are you today? We are going to take a little blood sample to make sure everything goes well".

I am afraid of needles of any kind and I know my wife is somewhat, but not as I am. I am a mouse with a big voice. I remember at one point prior to her treatment, she was sent to a department to have blood drawn. The technician that was administering drawing the blood could not fine a vein to draw. I was summoned to the tech office where she was. When I enter the room, tears were all over the place, her face I mean! That was when I become a little concern and said" Let us get someone else." That was a good suggestion for the young person wasn't experienced enough finding veins of patients with small veins.

They summoned someone else to comply and the job was done, and we waited a while for other testing.

You go to this place to another, where everyone looks like they are ready for heaven all. They all are dressed in white wearing smiles on their faces which give comfort to hurting faces. We chose a seat next to the window overlooking the lake gazing the ducks, and the waves floating back and forth, viewing the sun as it reflects on the blue water.

What was exciting for me! They served all kind of refreshments of cookies, candies, colas, and many good things. I got in the habit as we waited in the waiting area; to want to move things along in a faster pace to get to the department I love.

Finally, we gotten a little better of the drill each day for four days a week, either in the early mornings we were to be there.

We would spend about three hours in that facility sometimes she would sleep quietly, but not very long she was to concern and I knew this than to fully rest.

I must admit there were days I should have stayed home it was getting a bit on my nerves seeing this day in, and day out. The cocktail they give are reddish and flowing into the veins. Daily we waited to hear things was getting better as we joined in prayer with other surrounded us whom we knew needed our support too.

I understand what David speaks about in the valley of the shadow of death" When you are going through something that you think no one else is going through, think again! That valley is not friend to anyone. The shadow itself is fearful, it is not death, but the thought of dying is frightening.

You see so many others around you so broken and weak. Many have no love one to visit them or to sit with them, other do not have children or relatives to come and share a moment. Yes, the valley is frightening and dark and lonely. But even is the darkness moments David concluded "I shall dwell in the house of the Lord forever. Psalm 23:1).

After considering what she had to go through, my condition was much easier as I watched. She really had to have more given, making sure things would go in the right direction. I could see in her eyes the sadness and gloominess taking on her life that bothered me somewhat.

Tiredness played a big role from the treatment she underwent. Again! It is not a small matter taking certain treatments, by the time we gotten home, she would be drained and feeling weak or tired.

This however; takes away strength you have to offer her; she would need reassurance that everything going to be fine. However; you'll not the fearful, and full of resolutions one, you are the giver and the giver must give" all they have, and sometime be met with oppositions.

Sometime! You think you have given your best that's not enough, you must find enough strength to finish the requirements desired. You do not leave the room, go to the store two often, this is another void to be filled. The floor needs cleaning, or the trash need emptying, the dog needs to go outside, the job is round the clock duties.

All and more tender care are needed when a person is faced with a threaten disease and there's no correct answers. Don't expect too much rewards for your services, it is mandatory to be there, to offer support and comfort.

As well I think I can prepare a meal, think again! It has nothing to do with the food you prepare it's more about the taste buds, and picking the right food wanted.

Nothing in the way of food, could prevent the taste of chemical in the mouth, the glands want the aroma of good food.

Don't take this as an offense jester; it is simply the way it works when one is unsure about many unclear pathways and the brain is full of chemicals. It is a brain that does not function as some usual thinkers thinks. However, speaking of my wife, she knows most things I had forgotten. Men remember, women have a great gift of remembering all the things you did right or wrongly. They specialize in things you forgotten after years.

These are days when your commitment is on trial. It will bring out the real meaning of staying power, to work through with your spouse. If you have children with other obligations their time must be divided with family obligations. Rightly so! Their lives must go on from day to day. If you are the only one where the burden must rest, be prepared to have challenges, we as men must rise to the occasion.

What I learned through the process, the nursing facility was where the majestic ordeal really begun.

When we arrived at the clinic there, a friendly staffer greeted us waiting with open hearts to assist us in whatever way they could. I could see the care and support, the skills displayed in handling each case that was presented.

They were full of smiles, and encouragements endeavored to ministers the faith, making fun with joy with each person kindly, displaying a sense of responsibility tirelessly.

I loved the cookie cart that came around; this was the moments of retirement, and relaxation, only for a moment or course! But it seems to have lasted for months.

There also, the doctors would come around to check the patients whom was injecting or receiving chemo. Mainly they were making sure the right amount was administered. If that part was completed, you are assigned to make your visit to the x-ray personnel.

Also, they would need to develop the right marketing to apply the x-ray that it wouldn't affect other part-that did not need that application.

They often told you what the risk administering the x-ray into the body, and the effect and what you can do to make the process a little easier.

One of the parts I enjoyed was, I was given the task to apply a medication to my wife with a needle, each and every morning where it was needed.

Doing those times, I could practice my medical skills, and felt I was making some worthy contribution sticking her with those kneels. It was a pat on the shoulders which I gave myself, knowing this would give her some release before going to bed each night.

One of the things they informed their patients after taking chemo is, the possibility of loosing your hair! I thought to myself "Wow! This stuff is ruff" and that it was. A few weeks after taking the medicine surly enough! Small portion of hair began to shed, and this was not good for a woman who knew her hair is her crown, but she was very cute.

I would catch her starring in the mirror while asking me "do you see any hair coming out? At times I would say no! To protect her emotions knowingly she was facing another unwanted condition.

Having been a barber over forty-two years I could see the declining or reseeding of the hair line. "Are you telling me the truth she asked? Not much! Just a little here and there I would say'.

She knew it was, but she was asking me to conform that it is so! I think! But she wanted to know how I will deal with it. She had forgotten over the years I have styled many women heads baldness. At the time I did not know why they wanted to cut off such lovely strings of hair. Little did I know why many women wanted to have their hair cut very short.

I am aware more than ever! not all the times it's about woman wants to resemble men with short hair,
they have other issues we sometime do not understand.

We must be careful not to judge others so quickly, there are million of people out there are facing life threaten problems and many takes fro granted.

Finally, she decided to let the professional barber do the honor. Talking with her and reassuring her all is well bald or not I have your back" I said, she has a perfect round sculpture. She really looked great! Like when we got married in the sixties when most young ladies were wearing their hair cut very low.

We had difficulties many times dealing with what is known by many "the chemo brain" I did not know what that meant but soon found out.

Seriously! It is a fact you must know this and what it does to a person mind. The least thing you say, or don't say become a matter of a seriously war battle. This is not a short battle; this battle goes on for some time.

It was one of those things you had to learn what has taken place in their body. I tried all that I could to bear the better words that would not cause a conflict.

It was like another person has entered the body and you must stay on alert, with a governed tongue, and a watchful eye making sure you don't lose a tongue, and both eyes removed.

I take seriously what James the apostle meant! "Even so the tongue is a little member and boasted great thing, Behold, how great a matter a little fire kindest! (James: 3:5, 6,).

Yes; we men of Mars keep in mind your spouse is from Venus. It is a fact not only when she is facing threaten issues, this is a fact in real life. "What a different a word makes!

There are flames that will blaze up in your life often taken for granted, Or, course one will not know this unless, you are forced to fine out for we, by walking in the foot prints of those gone before you.

Quilt is the master of all flames. It is that feeling someone is the blame when living closely with someone you love. The desire is to get them healthy as soon as possible. Even is the midst of guilt coming, fear, and even doubt that this is not going to work as one desire to think. Questions arises throughout the mind what can you do more for a faster recovery?

I remember hearing her say to her God, "Why me! I responded "why not you? She was full of self approval. She had her own slanderers the way things ought to be. I knew well about this as a minister, we strive to please Him, and there are times it seems he went into a far country and no where to be found.

At one point! In my life as a young minister I had that all self appraisal until, God allowed me to fall flat on my face. Through the eyes of my youngest sons, at birth he had a light surrounding the cliquey that was bright. His eyes had a light glow appearance about both eyes. My wives notice it and brought it to my attention, which reminded me that as a small child amazing miracle are displayed. It was nothing the child had done that gave such radiant light, but the simple appearance of the glowing was real. Let us confess, we all have thought we had matters in our control when we were young and stupid. Our self-righteousness was at best the better than most. We heard not, we did not, we sort not, we asked not, until we have not other options.

I had to study myself, going back turning the pages of my life, searching all that I did and that I did not understand why, I did whatever, constantly blaming myself repeatedly, and again.

"What I did or did not do had anything with this-disease, to be attractive to me? Slightly ignoring what my siblings have gone through, added more self infliction self guilt. I was responsible for what is happening with me. I knew I could handle this! I am a man, and had God on my side anyway, it does not seem right.

I had my work cut out for me considering what my wife maybe thinking. We loved God and had given our life to Him at an early age. We had pastured many churches seeing others healed through the power of God.

I would tell her, "You know Jesus did no harm but took upon himself our sins and guilt and bored it upon the cross? Why did God allow His son to suffer and to die having a sinless life?

Just think about that for a moment! If he spared not His Only Son and allowed Him to become a curse for us why are we so much the better? "He that spared not his own Son, but delivered him up for us all, how shall he not with him also freely give us all thing? (Roman: 8th,).

One thing for sure, God through the Holy Spirit was speaking in my heart words that I often spoke but did not realize what dept and power they had in our lives until we were faced with uncertainty.

Your mortality comes right to your face when you are face to face with cancer. Cancer had no certain person whom it will or, will not attack. We can cry out like, Isaiah cried! "Woe is me! For I am undone" (Isaiah: 6: 5,). You may see an imperfect human in the presence of a Holy God.

This does not happen to a great deal of folks, for many folks do not consider God to be the head of their lives. They may not have any church affiliation, or attend church, as often as others do. Many do not regard God as their Lord, and Savior.

However; those of us who have a relationship with Him remember! Our live can be a testimony for those who suffering around us, and we can be a light in dark prevailing times.

This happened many times as we sat in the operation room, in the chemo room, and as we talked to those who had no hope, God gave, us a message not for ourselves, but for those hurting and needed hope.

We must keep in mind, what is takes place in our lives are not necessary for us. Therefore, the call is much higher, and larger than those of us who are also dealing with life flames. We dare not pity ourselves there is to much work to be done.

While contemplating over the scope of things that had taken place a few months ago. One would not digest what takes center stage next. Getting home after work, the phone ranged on the other end was my brother calling from New Jersey. Hello bro, I said! Hello, he replied; you know your sister passed! What! I said when? You'll kidding What happened.? All I was told she was sitting having a birthday celebration with her grandchildren and passed out is all I heard. We knew she had been in and out the hospital over some time, but never to the point we would experience death at such an early age of sixty is to young. It is only three of us sibling remaining, and I never thought we would out live our youngest sister. She had four children whom could give information as to what happened. I called to get the important information as to what happen. All we learned she was sitting and enjoying the afternoon with her grandson and leaned over and admittedly passed away. A week or so prior to her passing, we spoke with her by way of the phone and we told each other, how much we loved each other. and I will give her a call later. Well; later, never came, but only, when I eulogized her remains recommended by the family. This is a flame that resonated deep within our hearts. Yes, we all have misfortunate situations in all our lives. Different things happen to all of us, we ask ourselves, "how long will this storm continue? How long will we must continue, with suffering and pain? I remember a saying by the apostle Paul who was lying in a prison cell writes, in one of his's letters to the Philippians church, stating," But I would you should understand, brethren, that the things! which happened unto me have fallen out rather unto the furtherance of the gospel. [" Phillippian1:12,).

We are God's handiwork, we are God's property, we can take our life and understand that God will use us with sickness, and weakness.

Many times, it is good to be unable for us to fix our own problems; if we attempt to do this we are not allowing God, to use us for His own glory. We belong to Him, and he certainly knows what to do with us, even if we expire in the process.

Paul the apostle made this statement, "For to me to live is Christ, and to die is gain" (Roman: 1,).

There is a song my father and mother sang often in church, and at home as we sat around or working. "Must Jesus bear the cross alone and all the world go free? No! There's a cross for everyone, and there's a cross for me. This consecrated cross I bear till death shall set me free, then I'll go home my crown to wear, for there's a crown for me."

Cancer, has it power over our physical lives, but Christ has your souls in his care. Nothing can separate us from the love of God. "For I am persuaded that neither death, nor life, nor angels, nor principalities, nor powers, nor things present, nor things to come, nor height, nor depth, nor any other creation, shall be able to separate us from the love of God which is in Christ Jesus, our Lord. (Roman: 8,).

Yes, we had the flame of "Cancer, and there are million of others who are facing this disease daily. We have seen small children, babies, whom haven't lived long, teenager's black, and whites, rich, and the poor, who are living with no hope. When there is no hope, you see no future, and when you see no future, your life is doomed.

None of the material things you have or wishing to accomplish means anything. When your life in turned upside down, your financial status is on the blink, we must come to some conclusion, there must be a better way.

Where one lives, have knowledge puff up to the ceiling, whatever you may have material, cannot and will not give life and peace.

It come bring happiness for a short season and to some they only desire a short season for they give up on hope and having faith toward the future. Often many resolves before they search for extension of life is sought.

First fear grips the heart, and faith ceases, and hope dies and when one has gone this distance to not live for tomorrow, nothing can do them any good. Faith sees further than the presence. Faith looks beyond circumstances and obstacles and build realities, while doubt prohibits that view of hope.

One had to look deep inside and at least believe in yourself that there is something within that has the option to at least allow yourself to investigate your own reasons why not allow yourself a chance for tomorrow things can rapidly change if you make the right choice to act.

So what! If you fear what had taken place? Think of others who are pleading for you to live and socialize with you and to build a stronger relationship even if you consider yourself mishaps. Most people whom had been considered mishaps had outgrown those who thought they weren't.

Problems are for champions not for whelps. Whelps do not challenge high mountains, or swim deep seas, or go to the highest space in the heavens they stay on local grounds. When you are at your lowest you are in a place to begin to build and reach for height above your saturation which calls out to you come!

Look at it this way for most of us whom has raised small children. We call them when they are young notice how they response. Come get up here! Or go there! Notice how they want to satisfy your bidding?

It is so when other want to see you healed and in good health. You may think that because you are in such state, that life has come to an end. Should you throw up both hands and wane without taking an account of yourself? Take notice! There are others looking on and taking notes how your response with your conditions. They might be adjusting themselves knowing they too might be going through the very same ordeal without mentioning a word. Just waiting to hear of your victories in faith and endurances you endured that bring light to their lives who are suffering.

Well! Go ahead and do that notwithstanding, you have some resources to start a new process with the help of those who care about your well being.

God does not give you anything if you refuse to accept his peace? He works like that. He says come unto me all ye that are heavy laden and burden I will give you rest" (Matt: 11:28,). You must take the offer if you want help you must take on the joke that is padded with His grace. This is a peace that surpasses all understanding as you attempt to solve it alone. A great deal of the time we have not because we ask not,' that is ask, seek, knock, do something at least if you can't be in the place you once were.

Some folk's lives are centered on things they have acquired and positions they have achieved. Only by surrounding and focusing upon those things that really matter, will change your attitude if those things become secondary, and your life is open for recovering a new lifestyle will take over.

Many like the comfort of living a defeated life style, they rather continue doing what they are comfortable with, than making the next move toward progress. In the natural life most folk's changes from one change of clothes daily. You do not put on the same piece daily. Those worn the day before need a fresh wash, and this allow for others to be used.

So it is in us! A change of a new prospective, a new thought, a new hopeless and faith, has in itself to change us and grant us hope that exceeds the routine of self defeat.

With such a large family from where I came from, there often seems never ever enough to go around. I often wondered what my father was thinking about. Or what he wasn't thinking about? Nevertheless! I am grateful to be a part of that family even in those difficult times.

What were they both thinking about as parents? Whether family planning was an option or not! They had a dream to accomplish their mission regardless what the outcome would bring them. They had meager resources, and whatever life throw at them, it was what it was and there was not other route around what was presented. Mother labored for ninny-nine months having her children. I am sure! There were things she wanted and need that would impact her life that would have made things a bit easily. She took what that she had and turned it into what she could do. That seems not the case today with the modern champs of growing a family today.

There seems to be an attitude of demanding and having control over matters as to predetermine the outcome and the future that all is well and adjusted. There is no need to worry about anything or have any disruption, and if it does not turn out the way planned then, life is doomed and damned. Every day they were working and facing hard challenges and life was distributing the word "not" or can't was the final result as time just kept moving forward.

Mom could have thrown up both hands and ran away somewhere to get some her sanity. Dad could have opted out early never to be seen again like many fathers does today with one child, and not sense of being accountable.

They didn't have medical facilities like we have today, Insurance O! No! no such thing in a small town and communities where only sick, and the suffering occupied. I never remembered any of my siblings going to see a doctor unless it was a matter of life and death saturation.

Folks back then pride themselves of having good neighbors, and family who worked together commanding and generating support for those whom has fallen ill, with what meager substances they gathered by the knowledge granny had cropped up or something their ancestries had passed down through generations was the medicine they used.

Folks were hurting, and had a shortage of supplies to go around, and hoped for anything other than death. Many want to live for something, then to lay on soft clean lining and complaint'. With our modern medicine and clean places, we dwell are among some of the best. We are blessed to have 911 calling assistance, all kind of protection services, and yet we complain "nothing is good enough".

Perhaps many! May have had cancer and didn't know it way back ago. My mother nursed most of her children and I don't remember her speaking about cancer at any time to of her siblings. Not saying it did not happen, just saying! She lived with a positive attitude about life and served her God.

What did happen then, then what is happening now? I mean; cancer is a big deal in this society. Everywhere I go, and most conversations daily, in the commercial displayed advisements, the cure for cancer is spoken about.

What do you think? I remembered growing up we had a vegetable garden everything we ate come from natural growth. The food tasted differently even if it was cook with port lard. I mean full of that stuff in most every meal. There was no Crisco, or corn oil of the lack in preparing a meal.

As African Americans they all ate parts of the animals not necessity the good parts like, chicken necks, liver, bowls which is the intestines of the pig. Or course many folks will not admit it. I am willing to share our specialty diet with anyone for it kept us alive.

We drink well water dug by our fathers or men in the community. We used out door facility as a toilet, in the rain, or cold weather. We lived in houses with no installation practically on the ground as some would have it, yet men and women lived a long life.

Today we have all the modern facilities all over the planet, we use all the modern equipment and yet, million are falling away from the moral fiber of making our society better for themselves and others. Many are driven toward a selfish or self-centered life, which describes an attitude of entitlement. Years ago, we that are over sixty years of age could not express such desires in the same manner as our younger generation does today.

We were taught that, "No one owes you anything! If you want anything you must to work for it, Life does not come on a silver platter!

If were sick "you must seek to get well" You cannot give in to your self pity, and depend on others to succumb to your desires, and wants.

You must give those working with you something" that will help in searching for answers for your conditions; you cannot have it your way.

We must face the fact of life, which we all should be working for the advancement for all of people, there are folks who are hurting, and hungry, going without every day fighting, and struggling to put out flames of fires that blazes up.

Many are paining and are facing some unusual circumstances finding them dealing with issues not in their strength to quench such oppositions. Many are working to work, and others are working to live, and some finds it a pleasure to work for things that temporarily vanishes. While others are busy working just to survive each day to provide a simple meal, or clothes, shelter for themselves and families.

What happens when life has taken away all the security you felt you have achieved by working only for things? While on the other hand, if things are taken away at the spare of the moment, you were depending only from day to day for your survival which one has the greatest concern? The emphases should not be placed on the things we possess, but rather on the things that will endure through eternally. We should always be driven to expand upon loving and caring for those so hurting.

When they realize that material is taken away, what they have left to satisfy their longing? Which one of these hands would you prefer? A willing hand of one that is full of a little love or a hand of an individual filled with gold that is poison?

There are those who work to live with the risk of taking the hands of poison to have it for such time they have determined. There are others who are willing to risk taking what they can do for others without risking their entire life for that which counters fit in nature and limited. The fowl of the air grants us the opportunity to understand the meaning of a fulfilled life. The little sparrow puts no demands on themselves about the burden of tomorrow, yet, they fly freely taking care of their responsibilities.

So how much more should we be concerning our plight? We are all living on borrowed time that runs it course. These are they who prioritize the real meaning for living they have chosen to be a channel for others who need deliverance for the flames of destruction. They are willing to take the place of those who are hurting, and become a channel, assist in diminishing fires another encounter.

Restoring life and giving back to someone their self-respect and restoring dignity to someone whom has fallen in the flames, who only need kind words to lift themselves from some slippery slopes of life.

On our way throughout life, we may have met people who did not appear to us as hurting or broken. Often times they do not display such conditions of suffering. Many are subdued quiet, not verbal who at times stand alone are working or playing that appears healthy.

Many we may assume live in large mansions, drive expensive automobiles, they have achieved success, and greatness, but is concealed in a bottle with broken pains and hopeless.

Smiling faces and hurting hearts, which are full of allusions and frustrations. Yet, amid such display and hidden beneath the glimmer, and glamour, are individuals living in a desert storms without any solution in focus.

They specialize in camouflaging their identity because of the inner conflicts has stiffened that freedom of expressions. They live with unresolved notions making their lives acceptable concealing inner conflicts trying to handle things on their own.

If you have not visited our nation facilities it is advised to do so, its offers reality of many who has no other choice but to be there. They are there seeking advice while listening and adapting to the environment and elements that may give release. It is a wonderful facility doing hands on hands administrating the important work assigned to their hands helping others who cannot help themselves.

These are men and women of faith bending toward those whom seem helpless and building lives. I considered the boldness of each as they await the magical hands approaching to minister support. I see the smiles, revealing on the faces, that life and restoration is finally coming to restore that which they lost. When the body suffers there is a sense of weakness, of being dismantle associational with the same body once you had. Anyone and anything that seems to offer solution to the problem is welcome.

At the same time when they realize there is a cloud of supporting doctors, nurses, and family member, and friends, the light began to shine through from disparity to dignity. I understand like most," People needs people" These are healthy hands and minds, working magically united to mend the broken hearts and the wounded.

There are times in our lives that life will bring us face to face with our own reality. There are millions of wise men whom think, they have the keys to unlock all doors. But, there is a reality to have humility to be humble, and summit to the will of the Holy Spirit who can only help us to face our mortality when we are in our flames of despair.

It is within all of us to boast about the good times we experience when things are going well with us. Suddenly our life is derailed by something that is so unusual transpire in our lives. It catches us off our guards, it brings to us a sense of lost, and wonder.

We feel disarmed insecure, the quaking beneath out footage or bridges are crumbling into deep waters and we are without life supports. Our natural habitats or our cockscombs, are no longer our safe havens, and our nests are invaded after all that we claimed is no longer there.

You are now shocked and dismayed that it has happen to you like millions you passed on the streets as you went without notice of them daily. You are now in the reality of something "strange and it is disturbing and fearsome as you contemplate what to do next?

There are natural things around us they are for our good they are what they are described to be "natural". But there is another force given to believers to have within it is called the Spirit of God.

When one recognizes the new life that dwells within them, that is the new birth that is given to us when all other powers have failed. Christ has come to indwell within us to help and guide us and teach us, when the chips are down.

Whatever, and whoever we may think we are we are not such a great person until the indwelling Spirit takes over from the inside out. He is free to all that calls upon Him to make intercession for them when all other powers has fallen.

That natural person we have being depending upon is now weak, failed, and broken needs that which is larger than medicine, and doctors. I believe God uses all these instruments to aid in our diseased bodies. Even though- regardless of age and culture, and religious practices, when the flame of cancer sticks, we all seek deliverance regardless from where it comes.

You may have thought that your flames could never be blown out! Like the titanic, "it will never sink". You have a good family history; they all attend the church every Sunday. You have wonderful families all which are well while rubbing shoulders with the great, and the good and smiling faces.

Let me say it for you! It means nothing when you are brought to your mortality with an illness that is undesirable. It has a tag or labor written on it" I am a life killer".

You are stopped in your tracks gazing in the far distance considering, what options you should take to prevent this invasion within the body. Most times one cannot feel cancer, it is a silent and evasive disease that does not carry pain an alarm doesn't necessarily go off, "You have cancer! This comes by check-ups, and other necessary things we do at one time of another from those who specializes in medicine states.

These are men and women across out spectrum that has acquired the knowledge and been in testing that has determined the nature of this disease. The subject matter in a topic we have discovered in these later years is massive. A commercial has increased and marketing this disease over the news networks is doing a large job trying to inform us of this disease before hand.

The health department are spending millions alerting the nations of what this crawling monster if bring home to millions. This is disturbing and can cause an emotional stress in our lives as we attempt to buy products and eat the right foods to help our bodies. This is when we come to question our mortality because of the unknown of what and how this could happen to us!

After a while of contemplating and deep concentration over such matters, the pain and fear of the unknown pushes a study hand reminding us of how fail we truly are. There are times when there is no anxiety form of suffering but on the inside, we are facing a serious problem. We ask ourselves "Is this the end? Is this the conclusion of my existence here on earth? Saint or no saint, we as humans must come to some conclusion about our end in this life if you really must conscious to face up to it.

Visiting one of the medical facilities where chemo is applied to patients some gentlemen came in we considered very proudly walking and somewhat argon saying" bring it on" meaning give him all that they have he could take it. After many visits later, we say him in a fever able state weakly and frail. I wasn't sure he knows what he really speaking about hiss ability to handle such treatment! Seriously he did not for the medication have gotten his better part of his body and he was in a humbling state of mind.

As a Christian person I knew quite well that's my attitude I thought one should present when he or she is relying on the creator to have the final say. If there is going to be any healing, it certainly must come from God the given and substance of life to overcome this illness. If He chooses to take our life then, so be it for He is the giver and keeper of our lives. I will not play superman in the moments of humans' weakness! There are things in this life regardless whom you are, will straddle your faith, and challenge your thoughts. I am reminded of our Lord before going to the cross how he cried out! "Father, if thou be willing, remove this cup from me; nevertheless, not my will, but thine, be done" (Lk. 22:42). He has the power to change your thoughts, and fill you with strength, He loves you so much and you cannot change that regardless how you may feel about that. Remember in scripture, the Lord asked Ezekiel an important question. "Son of man, can these bones live? And I answered, O Lord God, thou knowest he replied."(Ezekiel: 3,). It is smart to allow God to answer His own questions if you do not know the answer. He made the bones and persons, why wouldn't He know how to put things back in place

We visualize our final end with cancer spread all over our bodies or in certain places within our bodies regardless! It is there, and you are alone dealing with it. Who cares? It's your body and your situation. What can you do about it? If you could do anything to change it, you would. But, no! Either you wait and seize and wait and cry and know no reason why! It just happens.

Chemo takes toil on the body; the fluid runs through the veins throughout the body is said. The medical community describes it as a poison solution that attacks the cells of cancer and that it does.

Who would ever think that such a chemical could heal that disease? I know for sure having dealt with it personally; it weakens the body to a certain degree. This red substance appears dangerous as it is released into the vain, but it has worked for others it can help you too.

Can one survive from it? Yes, we have a testimony you can recover and be stronger again. Time is of the essence to wait and watch moments is ever not fast enough. You may feel like a leaf handing from a tree, just dangling by the wind of change. One moment it a cool breeze, and another moment it is a hot blistering sun, changing your moods daily.

The tiredness and sleep derivation is tossing and turning during certain periods is something you seem to never get over. The emotional stress the feeling of emptiness and frighten, is part of our simple frame, we are but humans. Amazing! You will discover a humbling experience regardless of what state you find yourself. No finance, no home security, not saving bonds, any material things can give you the satisfaction you long for and that is, and the words you'll free.

Different individuals experience different results. However; this is the road one must travel in the process since all is do to something you cannot do alone. It is so important to have loved ones around if you have any. No those who see and seize with guilt, and remorseful dispersions. You need faith people surrounding your crib or bedsides bring good tithing of great joy. You should not get weary even though you want to throw in the towels or strike out at anyone who mean well in your process.

I know men especially have tried to fix it themselves with other devices and hearsay solutions. Many have tried to extent the process by mere changing the mind that it is not so. Regardless whatever you think other than visiting your physician, you are making a big mistake. Sure no one wants to lose what many think their manhood but if you have any such things it must be dealt with right away or there will be no man around.

An often man by nature likes the idea of challenging life to find out later, it is not in their hands alone to resolve such issues. However; we have dominion over certain things on this earth but, we must do it by working together with those who are skilled in knowledge and training.

Even though I have faith and has my agenda what I believe. I must recall that faith without works is dead being alone. "What doth it profits, my brother, though a man says he hath faith, and have not works? Can faith save him? (James 2:14,).

There are men whom are used as instruments of God to investigate that which is beyond our understanding. They are given to us and for us, to help in the process of healing.

Time and time again! Over and over, there are those whom refuse to quench the fires that are set in their bodies, you may experience a slow urination, or paining when you do. There maybe found blood in the urine, or stool, regardless! Men check this out at your nearest office.

Fires are elements that have a life of it own the flames are uncontrollable. It has its own way depending on the debris on the surface not to mention, the fast spreading of the flames of prostate glands. Get a clear understanding; try to solve the problem with your pride standing in the way.

When the winds become a part or combined with the fire it is no telling which way the flames may travel. This sure we know that we have saturation out of control, and we need assistance and a control environment.

We summons the right departments that specialized in that situation. They are specialists who are trained to clear away your doubts and set new direction for recovery. Not all times they get it right its all depends how long and how far the fire has traveled prior of your visitation to the office.

How long do we wait before we come to the realization that we all encounter flames of life? I assure you! no one person alive have not gone or now, going through something that is larger than what they can handle.

Where do you go for help? Do you know the right person or person to contact? Perhaps you can't obtain one in your saturation or cannot afford the cost for resolve. I do remember those flames of the passing of my siblings who, had to face the ultimate because the lack of, or not having proper understanding of medical insurance to quench the flames.

We are experiencing all sorts of flames in our so city today. Millions are losing hope for the future. We are giving in to any and everything to do it my way or the highway is flames that are setting ablaze for some later time.

The question maybe challenge" what are we to do about it? What routes to take to avoid the event we see as destructive for our way of life and future?

It appears we are on an ever-sliding path going somewhere to some ending point. This is either by designed or by our choices. Do we follow the path that is laid out for us in the biblical context of our belief system? Or, are we the designer and controller of our own destiny as creators?

Not only were they engulfed with cancer but, other flames of a brokered relationship, the lost of a love one, the failing jobs, or lack of financing, or at the verge of a divorce.

These are flames we all face every day in one fashion or another, this life is not a perfect life world. It is a challenging world. We must remember we are not whispering as we go, we are struggling as we do. The moment we come into the world, we are delivered into hands of bitterness.

There are some things that is never full, look at some examples, an empty glass, the grave, the heavens, and the life we live are never complete. Life seeks to be complete in all parts. The voided space in our homes seeks to be filled with something we attempt to fill that void.

Can we replace all things as they were? I remember my childhood life which seems to me to be the most rewarding life I even knew. It was a time I felt close to the creator and all the things that were made wonderful.

Just smelling the soil, or viewing the rain fall, or the wind blowing across the plain are time I really enjoyed the best of life. Innocent you my say, I think you are right! My dependency depended on others whom had provided for me as I could rely on that as a new comer.

Being a novice is not a bad thing correct? Only if we

could just stay that way throughout our lives, this is not the big plan however. We come to continue to finish a work assigned by the architecture that placed in order a working universe. That is continuing evolving every second and minute, and hours of our lives.

We cannot alter such plan of the great and might sun shinning with such great brilliance that gives light to our solar system. It offers warm raises for out crops to grow, and for our lives just from the sun alone.

This massive orbit or planet just keep blazing and giving out what it is designed for. Suppose it will go out! What effect would it have on the earth and those of us who are living here?

I am not a scientist but this I say! "I am grateful it. It is there, to warm and give light otherwise; our solar system would be dark and empty. I have experienced something that I am always happy to feel and appreciate, the light that brings light into our dark and sinister world the light of Christ that shines in every heart. (John:1: 2).

I am told that a certain number of earths like planets can go inside of the sun to make up how large the sun is. This planet lights the entire universe and everything in it gets it light from the sun.

Where do we get help in our times of dealing with our flames in life we face? If it is not cancer what else are we grappling with?

We all have flames and passions about certain things,

or persons, or about our final journey as we go throughout this life.

What are we to do about it? Again! There are some things we cannot handle.

I recalled in the Month of June of 2015 my wife received a call from our son who lived in Atlanta Georgia. I heard her say, Oh no! I asked her what the matter is. She said Daniel's house was destroyed by fire last night.

The first thing came to mind, "Did anyone get hurt? Are they all safe and did they get out live? The answer was yes! They all did. Tears began to flow down our cheeks thanking God that he spared their lives. Our grandchildren are safe, and the entire family is Okay.

As the story goes, they all were sleeping around three 0, clock in the morning the alarm went off and their dog began to bark. He arose from his sleep and realized there were smoke and flames shutting out from the lower level where they slept.

The children were in separate rooms as he rushed to each room awakened them and summoned them to "get and get out right now" the house is on fire. They all ran down the stairway to the outside of the premise on the street as they watch the house disintegrate into ashes.

The firemen and other rescue officials were on the scene doing all that could be done to save the property. After the fire had simmered down or considered out, they were able some later time to revisit the burned home.

This they did and upon visiting the rubbish burned out home. A few years back I had given him a special bible my mother gave me to study from time to time. Being away from home for some time, I wanted something that reminded me of home.

When our son visited us in St. Louis, Missouri I handed him the bible and told him to read it and learn from it. He received it I not sure with reservation or not. I know he did receive it. The story that he told came from a deeper meaning of all the tragedy happened.

Receiving a call as he spoke with his mother whom was very concerned about his state and after a long conversation we both was on speaker phone. He said, "Daddy I have something to tell us" Okay I replied. "You know the bible you gave me from your mother? Yes, I remember! I found it within the burned house it did not have a scratch on it.

Right then, my wife and I praised the Lord knowing God was in the flames of fire, who led our children out through the flames.

This is the way they had to get out of the house. They had to come down the stairs to the lower level of the home burning to get to the front entrance. His office stood right in front another stairway. They had to turn left to go onto the outside to safety.

My wife and I looked at each other, saying" That was nobody but God He's the one that miraculously brought you to safety".

It doesn't matter if one refuses to believe it or not, we believe in the hand of God who performed the escape route. We believe he can keep that which we have committed to Him until the end.

It was easy for me to give up, and call it quits when I was diagnosed with cancer. I could have thrown in the towels as some would say. Sure, there was moments I got a bit discourage when I was told I had prostate cancer.

Did I fear at times? Yes! Fear will grip anyone when that word is pronounced. There were moments I thought about my death, and leaving my family and friends, departing this-life not seeing my grand-children grow up. Watching my youngest son wrestle with his young family, those are times you evaluate and considered how wonderful life is whenever you are face to face with cancer.

I cannot explain why I was left here but, this I know, God only knew the future that later my wife down the road would need help through the ordeal forth coming.

Ten years later she was diagnosed with cancer and she questioned why? Thinking to myself I said, Why not! So many others had danced with the music, what is our time all about?

I might have voiced this out loudly! It was a deeper meaning to that statement. What was God up too?

What is the lesson He want to get across? Certainly, we had no idea what he was doing.

As the conversation goes she mentioned many times to me" I met Him face to face as I lay on the couch. He pulled up a chair and talked to me. "Wow" he did that I said! She continued making her claim saying "God knows how to get your attention!

I kept reminding her in my statement that God said "everything is going to be alright, stop worrying I said, I knew worries only prohibited God's plan. Worry is like a rocking chair, it goes back and forth never taking you anywhere"

It can be described as a double standard, believing one things and doubting the same you want to happen. It's a sea wave that has no form, it can take you anyway, and anyhow without a solid guide or trust.

Humility is a good place to start out first and foremost, before a Holy God both of us took a new perspective focusing over the years of our life and what had taken place on our journey.

There were questions that came to mind as we searched our thoughts, why both of us received cancer. I cannot explain I am sure there are other cases of both husband, and wife had to deal with the same issues.

We tried not to force our religious beliefs nor justify them to others, but we would travel back through the pages of our lives and question "where did we go wrong, and what didn't we do to contribute to the cause?

I am dumb founded as to why, and who, and what it's caused it to flame up I know this! It is here, but not to stay, as I stated within my spirit, by life or by death, in the final and scope of things, we are more than conquered.

We attempted to deny it in some strange notion, but the professionals refuse to allow that. They told us we have the cancer and there is nothing to do but treat it and trust God.

The God part was simple to us, but the treating it was a different thing. This was a delicate moment in our life, just the thought of going through all the process.

So, we began to do the thing they told us to do. We began to comply with the rules of engagement. As we go and take the medicine and instructions, we kept trusting and joining in agreement day, and night's calling upon the Lord.

Yes! There were times when it seems He had gone on a long journey and we were in the flame of confusion while He waits behind the clouds.

Finally, thing began to come to mind what we had done in our lives, as we watch the hand of God working on our behalf.

Times like these will cause you to experience a renewal of God's favor not now you are facing some mishaps, but times looking back prior to cancer, how He had worked in other matters you forgotten about.

Don't forget the times when you are at your worst you needed a job, or food for the family, or a raise to secure your livelihood and were denied.

When your business was sinking in debt, and in a financial straight, or when your child was in the hospital and needed help.

The moment when you gave birth and your child was near death, or you husband was ill for a long period and you did not know how things was going to fare out? What it was that came in those moments that changed that situation in your life? Those things were as important as anything else. Any of us can lose things that are important as cancer, if they are not restored. Cancer was our enemy! Was that something we did not feel as pain, we only knew that it existed within our bodies? We understood quit well what it could do, and what it had done. It was to both of us a burning ever continuing flame we realize what going on with others we spoke with in the centers we visited.

I can name much saturation by the thousands, which have experienced some kind of "flames" and disappointments. Living in the inner city for some part of my personal life, I say and experienced many flames" of fiery or emotional upheavals with occurred. From one day to the next you could visualize hopelessness', fear, rejection, the homeless, depravity, divisions, abandon housings, loneliness, sadness, fights, violence's all of which are some misfortune in the lives of many.

If you reverse that community and view it as the quite suburbs or rural communities, there is little different in either one.

Consider how the rules are applied by codes applicable for change, while a no coded is considered restricted or inapplicable. Therefore; all have same elements but applied in a different manner. How so? The one who lives in a deprived community viewed as the satirist the functional community is considered the "privileged community" whiles the dysfunction is considered the "none privileged" community.

All the things which occurs in the "none privileged communities are the same in the privileged communities.

In a quieter considered atmosphere as a controlled environment official of law uses an acceptable method than that of the lack communities. The law enforcers use other rules of engagement for the deprived, then that of a privileged community, differently.

However; under my view pain feels the same to all people regardless from where they live, or home they come from. The color of a man's skin does not protect him for the flames of life not one's finance, or his religion, creed, nor his ethnicity, or culture. Cancer has no respect of people's regardless weather they are, Whites, blacks, Hindus, Jews, and gentiles, Cancer does not separate the classes of suffering people. Regardless how far we travel, or fly or eating the right foods, smokers or none smokers, drinkers, or drunker s, all falls short dealing with such a harmonious disease. All deals with cancer this flame that is spread throughout the world.

These human flames are continuously getting larger and larger as if it a large uncontrollable fire that not anything can quench. As I mentioned fire has a charter about it can purify things, or it can destroy things. The main jobs for firefighters are finding the fires and distinguish them within their power. So, it is in the days of our lives from one thing to another we are putting our fires, from our hearts.

The firing in churches, the shooting on our streets, our youth and adults moral compass is being burned by the fire of acceptance. People has choices to make when it come down to reality there are certain things we must choose not to do to have a full and complete route ahead. We cannot understand all blazes that arise in our mortal lives, but we do know when they come alone, we must do our best to defame them. The shooting in schools destroying our children, is a flame of fires shooting in movie theaters, the rise of international terror, our moral compass has begun to blaze, another fire storm after another.

Are we there yet? Or should we cut our vacation short? No! We can take another route to avoid such attack? It may not be a popular choice, but it is worth the try. We must ask for some solution that will summons us to a larger bidding. The bidding to have compassion with our humanity, and not abuse it the way many have chosen, Our call to return to the Archbishop of our soul and offer to him our will to be submissive to His biddings.

I recommend we take the test, rather than let these fires continue to blaze, or we can take a stand for what we believer, and hack with the results. There comes a time when a nation or a people must take a stand for all that is good for the nation. That being said: the good for all humanity to come to the knowledge of the truth, that is only found in the love for God, and demonstrate the love for his humanity his people regardless whom they maybe.

We must come to grapple with this disease that is wiping and wearing us out. We have rights as believers and so do unbelievers. We all have a choice how we desire our lives to end either, reject hope, drop faith, give up without a fight? Why?

I do not recommend, nor do I imply anyone to be ye follow of me. But be ye follower of whatever master your life. Either material things, or Jesus Christ", Whatever governors your behaviors that's your master either way, you must make a choice if you haven't already.

As for me and my house, we will serve the Lord."

The ending story is a remarkable story of one's faith

displayed in real life when you are facing life flames. These young men were Jewish descendants which has their own worshiping community and the God whom they had pledge to serve.

They were met with other religious community of believers whom did not know their God Yahweh whom promised he would protect them regardless what's the circumstance maybe.

They entered a country where there were laws established that there was only one god and that person was a golden image. The images were many of sorts perhaps wonderful and tempting.

But; the law was established for everyone to obey regardless; they must have adhered to it by all means. They refused to change their belief to do other than what their God has promised. They took a stand even if it was punishment by a fiery furnace to anyone found not worshiping the golden image set up.

All three of them established a relationship to agree not to bowl or stoop to that degree to alter their conviction. Therefore' by not submitting to that decree of law the kings become very disappointed with them. For their punishment they were cast into a fiery blazing furnace full of heated flames. Chances after chances the king gave them but they refused to stoop to that level.

More anger from the king to heat the furnace seven times hotter than usually and had these three young valiant trusting believers in the fiery furnace.

This worried the king for he wanted to see if they were alive at a certain time. But to his surprise, when he took a view inside the furnace he discovered, four persons instead of the three thrown into the flames.

He asked a question! Did not we throw thee in the furnace? The attendee said yes! But I see four! Said the king, and the fourth is like a god"

They all stood on their convictions that their God Yahweh, will deliver them from whatever they would face in their lives.

If it is so, our God, who we serve is able to deliver us from the burning fiery furnace, and He will deliver us out of thing hand, O, king. (Daniel 3:17,).

Well! This is the surprise and the result of the power we have within us, we have the Holy Spirit sealed within us. We will be fired up and ready to go through the flames is you are committed.

Regardless by life or death, He will never leave us, not will he forsake us. "And I will pray the Father, and he shall give you another Comforter, that he may abide with you forever". (John: 14:16,).

So you are in a flame and it doesn't feel right to be in that place and at this time in your life. Rest your concerns God let it rain on the just and unjust.

He will protect you in any situation with what little strength you have; I realize it's not much in your thoughts. I say to you 'Wait" just a few minutes your time has come, and you will rise up much stronger, and wiser, and better once you have gone through the fire. Come with us and see for yourself you can endure just for a moment and tomorrow will be a better day .

Through the flames we survive"

The bible below was given to me as a gift from my late mother whom I gave to my older son as a gift. It was special to me and I wanted to pass it on throughout the family heritage.

In June 2015 their home burned during a fire the entire house was destroyed. He kept this bible in an office desk in the lower level of his home. On one have to go downstairs to exit the home just across a hallway to exit out the door onto the outside. They all were asleep on the second level in the home and when they were awakened by the home alarm and the pet dog that barked louder and awaken the family. He rushed to the three children crying out "Get out! Get out! There's a fire" the all rushed out and exited the front entrance onto the grounds. After the rescue officials arrived and diminished the flames and the house was total ruined.

A few days later they had to opportunity to revisit the rubbish. He was investigating the damage of their home went to the once was office and opened the draw of the office while everything around it was burned or destroyed. He pulled open the draw to the once was a desk and when it was open this bible appeared with no burns or smoke or water damage. He called by phone and was speaking with his mother and in the conversation as we both listen he said" Dad I want to tell you something I said Yes! You know that bible your mother gave you? I found it in the rubbish not a scratch or a burn or water damage was on it at all. My wife and I rejoiced for we interpreted this was the word of God that was protecting them during the fire.

This is a true story of what happened in Gwinnett County in Atlanta Georgia. The word of God will never be destroyed even if the bible is burn. However, in this case it was found alive during the fire and kept for future reading, and for generations to come. Yes, despite having the disease called "Cancer" you are not alone in the pain and suffering you experiences during your struggle. Sure, no one else can understand what you are thinking or feeling, the loneliness, the moment you wish anyone, or something could ease the pain.

It Appears You Are Out Of Your Body And Has Moved To Another Place In Life. You Ask Yourself Is It All Worth It? Taking The Treatments Of Moving On Beyond. Our Experiences Have Brought Us Closer To The Divine Hands Of The Almighty That Has Come To Us In The Midnights As Silent Breezes Passes By.

 Is this death? Is this my time? Will I get to see the morning? All these things come to mind.

Then we discover a still voice saying, "be still and know I am God". Yes, it is a Mosaic experience We can come through the waters that floods over our bodies and bring comfort to the acing soul. It is not the flame that is so large; it is our confidence to withstand the flames.

We should always remember we are not alone there is help amid the flames. Not everyone can see the miracle or the hand that soothes the flames. We must understand that life brings to all of us some challenges we must response to. Remember whatever and whenever and however your flame comes remember. We are more than conquered through Christ who loves us." Through the flames we survived."

The prayer and argument

"Oh, that I knew where I might find him! That I might come even to his seat! I would order my cause before him, and fill my mouth with arguments" Job 23: 3,4,

Job uttermost extremity he cried after the Lord. He was an afflicted man of God who longed to see his face, he did not plead to be healed but to see his face. He did not pray for his children to be restored from death, and his property given him back from his enemies. He first and utmost cried out, "Oh that I knew where I might find Him. In our most difficult moments this is our cry to our God. God's children always desire to rush home when life flames that they may run to his seat. It is the instinct of all gracious souls to seek shelter from all ills that comes to destroy us from the pain and discomfort we face. One that does not know his God always resent him when they are afflicted by God. He feels banded and seeks to flee from the present of the creator. It is the nature of all believers to seek refuge in the care of Him that created all that they have obtained and given. In the flames of cancer or any other illness will mount up in your life but cannot quench the flames without reaching the throne and him who sat upon it. You will not be contented until you have rest. We that know you will call upon him even though he has allowed affliction to come in your life. The friends of Job who came to comfort him did little or no good; they came to judge and to Counsel Job. He could have very much responded in some hope of their company, but they came to blunt the pain he experienced but could not give the satisfaction he needed. There are many miserable comforters who come only to say hello. Like many that visits us only come to put more salt into our wounds to inflict more pain with the flames we have. Many times, the trusting soul is left without the presence yet he is so closed "My God my God why hast thou forsaken me? God is secretly substantiating his people when they least sense his presence. Sometime a little while He seems gone, and another time very close and yet the believing soul in strengthen when you see a little light shinning through within our suffering, this is when we are at our best. In our weakest moments we fine our strength to trust Him more knowing He is with us in the mist of our flames. So, you are in darkness and light has hidden her face, and the bridge you are trying to cross seems to be falling apart. You seem to be sinking in the swift roaring sea, and the waves are overcoming your will to struggle any longer. You are in your flames that is raging high, and the heat is often nearing your will and desires to destroy you. Your nights are filled with suspense, and the day is far away. You wish for the morning to soon arrive and the day light will burst in with sun, instead of rain. Then just surrender and say yes! Here am I do as you wish, I will stand the presence of the Most High whom I know lives, and for me to live am Christ, and to die is gain. "Through The Flames we survived

[2]

There are millions of men and women searching for hope in our political social and educational, and religious institutions, all who are hurting, there is a way that has developed over three thousand years ago.
There was an old prophet by the name of Habakkuk the prophet who faced doubts as we do today.

Around, the 7th century B.C, He questioned, and doubts arose from his jealousy for the holiness and justice of God. He was perplexed over God's permission of evil in his time. Why did he allow an enemy to come and destroy the people? Yet during it all, He found clarity as God's hand is leveled against all that he had done. This what the prophet discovered.

He discovered A New Perspective: (Habakkuk: 2:2)

He discovered Patience (Habakkuk: 1:12)

He kept his eyes on the Promises of God, He was resolute in his God (Habakkuk: 3:18)

He found a place to Praise God during disappointment (3:3,).

He kept his faith during great ruins. He learned he must live by faith and be vindicated only by the justifier God himself. (Habakkuk: 3:18, 19,).

Many times, we are the blamers of God. Often, we seek reasons to condemn God for things that happen in our lives. This is a way to turn inwardly to our lifestyles, and things we caused, and the choice we make, and made, that is the result of our lives, not all but many.

We must learn to name our mistakes, and misfortunes, and call them what they are, most times we are not committed to endure what life throws at us we give up to soon, and committee too late.

Zephaniah reached higher when the nation became infested with uncertainty, when all the evils that came alone the way. He acknowledges God hides himself and He also protects in His own time. There is hope if men acknowledge and repent he will come through the flames that comes. (Zephaniah: 2:3,).

Because things are not quite so well during your fires, you still have an obligation to reach out to a higher power. More power than a ship filled with precious stones. He will restore you if only you give yourself a new perspective. Continue to have patience and wait on the promises God who has extension for you. Don't give in or give up, there is a light at the end of the tunnels.

Through all the flames that you are experiencing give yourself a new perspective, wait patience, believe in the promises of God.

This book is dedicated to the following:

SSM Hospitals in St. Louis City and Counties across the United States,

St. Joseph Hospital St. Charles, Mo.

St. Joseph Hospital Lake, Saint Louis Mo.

SSM Cancer center: Lake Saint Louis, Mo.

St. John Cancer Center Town and Country Mo.

The Doctors

Nurses staffers All SSM facilities

Friends and Family

And the faith communities.

I would like to you the reader write me a review to help me tell my story to others going through this life flame.

send me a short note: danj8447@gmail.com

Figure 1

---

[1] Like Moses standing at the ever-burning bush its flames never consumed yet! God's voice spoke and said to Moses, "take off thy shoes, for the ground you are standing on is holy grounds" I was not sure where we were standing, it seemed like quick sand. There was little hope of withstanding the slush beneath our feet, as gravity seems to pull downward on all.

[2] For those of you who are going through difficulties in life weather its cancer of just simple life experiences that is frighten.

You that are perplexed, engulfed with disparity, broken and shattered pieces, there is still a new day. I know you think the world has turned away from you. You are in a quite and lonely place wondering about the outcome of your sickness. You often think about your mortality, the leaving on a love one, small children, a, or wife, a son or daughter, struggling with financial strain, or incarcerated in some dark lonely place.

The economic issues, facing job layoffs, or and incurable disease, or hurting from the lost of a love one you are not alone.

THE TRAILING BOOK

The Verdict Of A Closed Case" By D.W. Jordan

ISBN: 9781622302062

Through The Flames We Survived' By.D.W. Jordan

ISNB: 8798642113790

ALL THESE EDITIONS CAN BE PURCHASED ON LINE AT THESE ONLINE SITES:

Kindle publishing/ Amazon.com/ Barnes and Nobles/ Wal-mart/ . In all book stores and online..

Thanks all for your kind sopport. I lost nine siblings of eleven. However, we have been able to give support to millions going through cancer. You can make it, you will be blessed to tell your story.

however

www.ingramcontent.com/pod-product-compliance
Lightning Source LLC
Chambersburg PA
CBHW070715250726
48662CB00001B/427